Crossway Bible Guide

Series editors: Ian Coffey (NT), Stephen Gaukroger (OT)
New Testament editor: Steve Motyer

Titles in this series

Luke:
Crossway Bible Guide

Simon Jones

Crossway Books Leicester

CROSSWAY BOOKS
38 De Montfort Street, Leicester LE1 7GP, England

First published 1999

British Library Cataloguing in Publication Data
A catalogue record for this book is available from the British Library.

ISBN 1–85684–190–1

Set in Palatino

Typeset in Great Britain

Printed in Great Britain by Caledonian International Book Manufacturing Ltd, Glasgow

CONTENTS

Six routes through Luke

1. Important themes in Luke's Gospel:

2. Discipleship as a journey:

3. The parables of Jesus:

4. Examples of faith:

5. Good news for the poor:

6. The prayer life of Jesus:

Welcome!

These days, meeting together to study the Bible in groups appears to be a booming leisure-time activity in many parts of the world. In the United kingdom alone, it is estimated that over one million people each week meet in home Bible-study groups.

This series has been designed to help such groups and, in particular, those who lead them. These Bible Guides are also very suitable for individual study, and may help hard-pressed preachers, teachers and students too (see 'How to use this Bible Guide').

We have therefore enlisted authors who are in the business of teaching the Bible to others and are doing it well. They have kept in their sights two clear aims:

1. To explain and apply the message of the Bible in non-technical language.
2. To encourage discussion, prayer and action on what the Bible teaches.

All of us engaged in the project believe that the Bible is the Word of God – given to us in order that people might discover him and his purposes for our lives. We believe that the sixty-six books which go to make up the Bible, although written by different people, in different places, at different times, through different circumstances, have a single unifying theme: that theme is Salvation. This means free forgiveness and the removal of all our guilt, it means the gift of eternal life, and it means the wholeness of purpose and joy which God has designed us to experience here and now, all of this being made possible through the Lord Jesus Christ.

How to use this Bible Guide

These guides have been prepared both for personal study and for the leaders and members of small groups. More information about group study follows on the next few pages.

You can use this book very profitably as a personal study guide. The short studies are ideal for daily reading: the first of the questions provided is usually aimed to help you with personal reflection (see 'How to tackle personal Bible study'). If you prefer to settle down to a longer period of study, you can use groups of three to five studies, and thus get a better overview of a longer Bible passage. In either case, using the Bible Guide will help you to be disciplined about regular study, a habit that countless Christians have found greatly beneficial. (See also 'Six routes through Luke' for methods of selecting studies if you do not intend to use them all.)

Yet a third use for these Bible Guides is as a quarry for ideas for the busy Bible teacher, providing outlines and application for those giving talks or sermons or teaching children. You will need more than this book can offer, of course, but the way the Bible text is broken down, comments offered and questions raised may well suggest directions to follow.

How to tackle personal Bible study

We have already suggested that you might use this book as a personal study guide. Now for some more detail.

One of the best methods of Bible study is to read the text through carefully several times, possibly using different versions or translations. Having reflected on the material, it is a good discipline to write down your own thoughts before doing anything else. At this stage it can be useful to consult another background book. See 'Resources' on page 14 and 'For further reading' on page 207. If you are using this book as your main study resource, then read through the relevant sections carefully, turning up the Bible references that are mentioned. The questions at the end of each chapter are specifically designed to help you to apply the passage to your own situation. You may find it helpful to write your answers to the questions in your notes.

It is a good habit to conclude with prayer, bringing before God the things you have learned.

If this kind of in-depth study is too demanding for you and you have only a short time at your disposal, read the Bible passage, read the comments in the Bible Guide, think round one of the questions and commit what you have learned to God in a brief prayer. This would take about fifteen minutes without rushing it.

How to tackle your group Bible study

1. Getting help

If you are new to leading groups, you will obviously want to get all the help you can from ministers and experienced friends. Books are also extremely helpful and we strongly recommend a book prepared by the editors of this series of Bible Guides: *Housegroups: The Leaders' Survival Guide* edited by Ian Coffey and Stephen Gaukroger (Crossway Books, 1996). This book looks at the whole range of different types of group, asking what is the point of it all, what makes a good leader, how to tackle your meeting, how to help the members, how to study, pray, share and worship, and plenty of other pointers, tips and guidelines.

This book is a 'must' for all leaders of small groups. It is written by a team of people widely experienced in this area. It is available at your local Christian bookshop. If you have difficulty in obtaining a copy, write to Crossway Books, Norton Street, Nottingham NG7 3HR, UK.

2. Planning a programme with your Bible Guide

This guide is a commentary on God's Word, written to help group members to get the most out of their studies. Although it is never ideal to chop up Scripture into small pieces, which its authors never intended, huge chunks are indigestible and we have tried to provide a diet of bite-sized mouthfuls.

If you want to get an overview of the Bible book in a series of meetings, you will need to select appropriate studies for each meeting. Read them yourself first and prepare a short summary of the studies you are tackling for your group. Ideally you could write it on a sheet of A5 paper and hand a copy to each member.

Do not attempt to pack more than one study into one meeting, but choose the crucial one, the study which best crystallizes the message.

If you do not intend to cover the whole Bible book, choose a series of studies to suit the number of meetings you have available. It is a good idea to use consecutive studies, not to dodge about. You will then build up a detailed picture of one section of Scripture. Alternatively, there are six suggested routes through Luke on p. 9.

3. Resources

You will find any or all of these books of great value in providing background to your Bible knowledge. Put some of them on your Christmas list and build up your library.

New Bible Dictionary or *New Concise Bible Dictionary* (IVP)
New Bible Atlas (IVP)
New Bible Commentary (21st Century edition) (IVP)
Handbook of Life in Bible Times, John Thompson (IVP)
The Bible User's Manual (IVP)
The Lion Handbook to the Bible (Lion Publishing)
The Message of the Bible (Lion Publishing)
NIV Study Bible (Hodder & Stoughton)
The Bible with Pleasure, Steve Motyer (Crossway Books)

The relevant volume in the IVP Tyndale Commentary series will give you reliable and detailed help with any knotty points you may encounter.

4. Preparing to lead

Reading, discussing with friends, studying, praying, reflecting on life ... preparation can be endless. But do not be daunted by that. If you wait to become the perfect leader you will never start at all. The really vital elements in preparation are:

▶ prayer (not only in words but an attitude of dependence on God: 'Lord, I can't manage this on my own')

▶ familiarity with the study passage (careful reading of the text, the Bible Guide study and any other resource books that throw light on it) and

▶ a clear idea of where you hope to get in the meeting (notes on your introduction, perhaps, recap what was covered at the last meeting, and what direction you hope the questions will take you in – don't force the group to give your answers).

Here is a short checklist for the busy group leader:

Have I prayed about the meeting?
Have I decided exactly what I want to achieve through the meeting?
Have I prepared the material?
Am I clear about the questions that will encourage positive group discussion?
Am I gently encouraging silent members?
Am I, again gently, quietening the chatterers?
Am I willing to admit ignorance?
Am I willing to listen to what the group members say and to value their contributions?
Am I ready not to be dogmatic, not imposing my ideas on the group?

Have I planned how to involve the members in discovering for themselves?

Have I developed several 'prayer points' that will help focus the group?

Are we applying Scripture to our experience of real life or only using it as a peg to hang our opinions on?

Are we finding resources for action and change or just having a nice talk?

Are we all enjoying the experience together?

What can we expect to learn from Luke?

What Jesus is really like

What the core of Jesus' message is

How Jesus brought good news to the poor

How we should live as Jesus' disciples

How to understand Jesus' parables

What we can learn from Jesus' prayer life

What money has to do with discipleship

What the kingdom of God is

Finding your way round this book

In our Bible Guides we have developed special symbols to make things easier to follow. Every study therefore has an opening section which is the passage in a nutshell.

The main section is the one that *makes sense of the passage.*

Questions

Every passage also has special questions for personal and group study after the main section. Some questions are addressed to us as individuals, some speak to us as members of our church or home group, while others concern us as members of God's people worldwide. The questions are deliberately designed:

 to get people thinking about the passage

 to apply the text to 'real life' situations

 to encourage reflection, discussion and action!

As a group leader you may well discover additional questions that will have special relevance to your group, so look out for these and note them in your preparation time.

Stop and look

This feature gives us the chance to stand back from the action and take stock. It gives a summary of what to look for in the passages we are about to read, and useful background material.

Digging deeper

Some passages require an extra amount of explanation, and we have put these sections into two categories. The first kind gives additional background material that helps us to understand something factual. For example, if we dig deeper into the gospels, it helps us to know who the Pharisees were, so that we can see more easily why they related to Jesus in the way they did. These technical sections are marked with a spade.

Stop and think

The second kind of background section appears with passages which highlight important themes or teaching. Bible references and questions will help you think them through. Write down your answers or use them as a framework for group discussion.

Has anyone got a map?

Luke was a travelling companion of Paul, an evangelist, missionary thinker and theologian. He wrote a two-volume work on the life of Jesus and the early church that we have in our Bibles as Luke's Gospel and the Acts of the Apostles.

One of his key concerns was to show that the church, which was growing rapidly in the early 60s when he wrote his two books, was the outworking of God's plan to bless the world through Abraham and his family.

By the time Luke wrote, Gentiles were filling the church and many Jewish believers were worried. Had God abandoned his people? In what sense was Jesus the fulfilment of Old Testament hopes for a Messiah? What was God up to?

Luke is concerned to show that God is being both faithful and consistent. He is being faithful to the promises that he made way back in history when he called Abraham and promised that salvation would come to the whole world through his family. He was being consistent in that his sending of Jesus was totally in line with what the prophets had foretold.

But as he wrote, not only were Jews outside the church opposing the message of Jesus as a 'heresy', but a fair number of Jewish believers were worried that the new movement had gone beyond its remit in admitting Gentiles to the fold without requiring them to observe Jewish dietary and religious practices.

It's for this reason that Luke has put together an account of Jesus' life that emphasizes his ministry to outsiders and his questioning of some of the practices of the Pharisees and religious elite in Israel that excluded ordinary folk from the benefits of faith. Although Jesus himself didn't have much of a ministry to Gentiles, Luke clearly shows that the prophecies around the time of his birth, as well as his practice of reaching the poor and marginalized within Israel, paved the way for the church's expansion into Gentile territory with a message that said salvation was found only through following Jesus.

So Luke includes many stories that the other gospel writers don't, because he's especially interested in how Jesus interacted with 'the poor' – a group that included women, children, tax collectors and others who were on the margins of first-century Jewish society. Only Luke, for instance, tells us about Jesus' healing of the woman bent double or his meeting with Zacchaeus the tax collector. Some of Jesus' best-loved parables are also found only in Luke – the prodigal son, the rich fool, the good Samaritan, the rich man and Lazarus, the unjust steward, the persistent widow, and the Pharisee and the tax collector.

A key part of Luke's story concerns how the disciples grew in their understanding of Jesus and his mission. Only Luke has an extended middle section in his Gospel telling the story of Jesus' journey from Galilee to Jerusalem (the so-called 'travel narrative'), during which Jesus seeks to mould his followers into a group that will be able to take his message to the ends of the earth after he has returned to heaven.

Luke tells his story in three distinct parts: the birth and early ministry (1:5 – 9:50); the 'travel narrative' (9:51 – 19:27) and the story of Jesus' death and resurrection (19:28 – 24:53).

THE JOURNEY OUT:
The birth and
Galilean ministry

Luke 1:1 – 9:50

Luke's story begins with a distinctly Old Testament feel – an angel appearing to announce that an elderly couple are about to become parents to a prophet. This is intentional. Luke is concerned at the outset of his account to show that the events he is talking about happened because God was working to a plan, a plan that was first announced to Abraham hundreds of years before and which was now reaching its crucial phase.

The two birth stories, with their many allusions to the story of Abraham and Sarah in Genesis 12 – 21, pave the way for the explosion of first John the Baptist and then Jesus into an Israel alive with hope and expectation that God will imminently act to set them free.

Jesus' ministry opens with a manifesto based on Isaiah 61 and delivered in his home town of Nazareth. This manifesto sets the scene for the whole ministry that Luke narrates in this opening section of his Gospel.

His story moves at a cracking pace. Jesus goes from village to village with some urgency, preaching the gospel, healing the sick and releasing those in bondage (all in accordance with his Nazareth manifesto). He also calls disciples to follow him – fishermen, tax collectors and others.

He encounters opposition too. The crowds love him. But the religious elite is at first suspicious and then openly hostile. The crunch time is coming, and Luke builds the tension through this first section with great skill.

The question hanging behind every encounter and piece of teaching is 'Who is this preacher?' The readers know, of course, because of the birth stories. But all the other characters are in the dark and have to work it out for themselves. The climax of the section comes in Peter's ringing declaration that Jesus is the long-expected and hoped-for Messiah.

But that's not quite the end of the section, because Luke paves the way for his long travel narrative by showing us that, though his disciples have some insight into who Jesus is, they are not yet ready to receive his mantle and carry on his work.

Luke 1:1–4

What kind of book is this?

Luke spells out how he has researched and put together his account of the life of Jesus and why it matters.

We all love a good story. In many cultures around the world there is still a strong tradition of skilled storytellers passing on the great truths of the tribe or nation to a new generation of eager listeners. Hollywood and the world's TV companies also know the power of a good story. And every year epic novels top the bestseller lists.

Luke has set out, like many before him (verses 1, 3), to tell us the story of Jesus. He's giving us a structured account of events that have taken place recently involving God and a carpenter-preacher from Nazareth in Galilee, and an explanation of what they mean.

He dedicates his work to Theophilus (verse 3). This Greek name means 'God-lover'. It is highly likely that he was a real person (otherwise Luke would not have referred to him as 'most excellent'). Judging from his name he was a Gentile. And it is probable that he was a relatively prosperous city dweller. He might even have been Luke's benefactor, the man who put up the money for Luke to publish his book. Of course, although dedicated to Theophilus, this book is for any who are interested in finding out more about Jesus.

Luke doesn't tell us why, since there are already so many books about Jesus, he's written another. It is possible he thought all the others were inadequate in some way. But this is unlikely, since it is clear that he knew what was in Mark's Gospel, and he included many of Mark's stories in his account in the same order as they appear in Mark. He did have stories that didn't end up in Matthew, Mark or John, many of which are included in his so-called 'travel narrative' (9:51 – 19:10; see p. 98); and he wanted Theophilus and others to read them.

It is also almost certain that from the beginning Luke set out to write a two-volume work: his Gospel and the Acts of the Apostles. His intention in doing this is clear: he wants to demonstrate that the God of Abraham, who promised that all the nations of the earth would be blessed through his family, has kept his promise. Hence the word 'fulfilled' (verse 1; see also the comment on 1:54–55). The good news is not just for Jews but for Gentiles like Theophilus. Everyone can find life and salvation through faith in Jesus. This is clearly spelled out in Acts, where the story moves from Jerusalem through the Jewish and Gentile cultures and ends in Rome.

Luke has gone about his task in the way a documentary film-maker might do today. He has found out about his subject by talking to people who met him, who were present at the events Luke describes ('eye-witnesses', verse 2). He's checked out the facts. It is quite likely that he visited some of the places mentioned in his Gospel. It is possible that when Paul, with whom Luke travelled, was in prison in Caesarea, Luke went across into Galilee and met members of Jesus' family and others who'd seen what Jesus had done.

But it is important to stress that Luke is not just telling a story like a novelist or TV journalist. This story changes people's' lives, because it concerns someone who is not just an interesting figure of history but who is alive today, and seeks the allegiance of all who hear his story. Theophilus, it seems, is already a Christian (verse 4), and Luke is writing to assure him that what he has already believed is true.

Notice that in his introduction, Luke doesn't mention Jesus by name. Already he is showing us that he is a master storyteller by drawing us in, causing us to ask questions about the tale he's going to unfold. What's it about? Who's it about? How will I fit into this story?

Luke whets our appetite to read on by telling us that what he's about to describe is the most momentous story ever told. He does this through his use of various words loaded with religious significance, such as 'fulfilled' (verse 1), 'servants of the word' (verse 2), 'certainty' and 'taught' (verse 4).

He also does this by emphasizing the reliability of the people he has spoken to. He hasn't just done a vox pop around Galilee asking passing strangers what they think of Jesus. He has spoken to those he knows were eye-witnesses who have since become members of the church (verse 2). These are people who have seen, pondered what they saw, stuck around to find out its true meaning and now live to pass on to others what they have discovered.

Luke's intention is that through reading his account of Jesus, people would not just be entertained or inspired by a ripping yarn about a remarkable man. He wants people to recognize what Theophilus already has: namely that this Jesus is the Son of God, the Saviour of the world, the fulfilment of all God's purposes for the world he made.

Questions

1. How did you first hear about the hero of Luke's story? Who told you?
2. In a world where there are many stories, do you believe that Luke's account of Jesus is true? What brings assurance that our faith is not self-deception?
3. What do you expect to find out as you read Luke's Gospel? Do you expect it to affect or influence the way you lead your life in relation to your family, to your job, to the world you live in, to God?

Luke 1:5-25

A messenger is promised

God puts everything in place for the fulfilment of his promise, starting with the coming together of the longing of a people for a Saviour and an elderly couple for a child.

Luke's story begins in the days of King Herod (verse 5), around 7–5 BC. But really it starts way back when God first embarked on his journey of salvation in Genesis 12. Although Abraham is not mentioned until 1:54, he lurks in the background from the moment the story begins. Zechariah and Elizabeth are childless (verse 7) as Abraham and Sarah were. Yet we know that Luke's is a story of the fulfilment of God's promises (verse 1). As Abraham was blessed with a son, so these verses are pregnant with the question: will Elizabeth and Zechariah's desire for a child be answered?

It does not look good. The couple are too old – as Abraham and Sarah were – and anyway, even when she was young, Elizabeth could not conceive. Both felt the shame of this in a culture that afforded greater status to households brimful with children. But they were righteous and devout (verse 6, with its echoes of Genesis 15:6; 18:19; 26:5).

Luke structures this story beautifully. It opens and closes in Zechariah and Elizabeth's home (verses 5–7, 24–25); the central action takes place in the temple, the centre of Jewish life and culture (verses 8–23); and at its heart is God's response to prayer (verse 13).

By the time of Zechariah there were so many priests that they had a rota for duties in the temple. He probably did two stints a year of a week each. As was the custom, each day one of the priests was chosen by lot to burn incense before the morning sacrifice and after the evening one (verses 8–9).

While Zechariah went in to burn the incense, the people outside in the courtyard were praying (verses 9–10). It is likely they were praying for the deliverance of Israel from her enemies; she had been under Roman occupation for over a century and was ruled by a hated client king. What they hoped for was a leader who was a cross between Moses the lawgiver, David the warrior king, and Elijah the prophet of the Lord. But was God listening?

In the sanctuary Zechariah met an angel (verse 11) and was terrified (verse 12). As is often the case when God responds to our prayers, we're thrown into confusion. This vision makes it clear that the choice of Zechariah to perform this special duty on this day was not an accident of how the lot fell; it was planned and brought about by God. Something momentous was brewing.

The angel tells Zechariah not to be afraid (verse 13) in words strongly reminiscent of God's promise to Abraham in Genesis 15:1, where God is reminding Abraham that he hasn't been forgotten. Then the angel says, 'Your prayer has been heard.' The question immediately arises: whose prayer? We've only been told of the people praying in the temple (verse 10), not directly of Elizabeth and Zechariah pleading for a child. The answer is that *both* prayers have been heard. For in response to the elderly couple's plea for a child, God is setting in motion the events that will lead to the deliverance of his people, and vice versa.

The angel spells out what Zechariah's son will be like: a mighty prophet like Elijah (verse 17); a servant of God filled with the Holy Spirit from before his birth, whose ministry will turn people around and prepare them for the coming of their Lord (verses 15–16); specifically one who will restore the relationship between fathers and their children (verse 17; Malachi 4:6). This rich phrase picks up the marriage between the personal and the global in this story: for just as Elizabeth's joyfully received son is part of the fulfilment of God's plan to bless the world through Abraham's family, so

27

the story that unfolds in the rest of the Gospel has to do with a Saviour who reveals God's father heart for lost individuals (especially in chapter 15) and who sent his Son to bring those individuals into the new family being gathered around him (see 19:10; Acts 2:38–42), a family that will be made up of both Jews and Gentiles – just as God had promised to Abraham (Genesis 12:3; Romans 4).

This episode ends with the contrasting reactions of Zechariah and Elizabeth. Despite all his prayers, Zechariah doesn't believe the angel (verse 18, echoing Abraham and Sarah's objections to God's promise in Genesis 17:17; 18:11–12). It is ironic indeed that a priest whose duties involve bringing God and people closer through the various offerings and prayers finds it hard to believe that God might actually respond to a specific prayer. For his unguarded words, he is struck dumb until the child is born.

Elizabeth on the other hand responds with faith and gratitude (verse 25). It is likely that she stayed secluded (verse 24) until her pregnancy began to show, so as not to draw the ridicule of neighbours who, like her husband, didn't believe what the angel said.

Here we have the first of many examples in Luke where a lowly woman upstages a male religious leader through her response to God. She is the model that Luke wants us to follow. But his story leaves hanging the question: how will Israel respond to this new move of God – with faith or with unbelief?

Questions

1. Is there a prayer you have been waiting for God to answer? How long will you wait?
2. Zechariah and Elizabeth's faith rested on the long history of God's dealings with Israel. Is it important for us to know about the history of the Christian church? Why? (If your group confesses its ignorance and wants to know more, why not plan a series of studies using *The History of Christianity*, ed. T. Dowley [Lion, 1977]?)

3. Do you think of the church as a global family? How can that sense of family be increased?

Luke 1:26–56

A Saviour is promised

For God's promises to be fulfilled, he needs people who will respond to his plans with faith. He finds a perfect example in a Galilean teenager.

 Events are moving quickly. Elizabeth is six months pregnant and it's time to tell another key player in the unfolding drama that her role is about to begin. The story moves to a girl as distant in status from Elizabeth as Nazareth was distant from Jerusalem.

Twenty centuries of church teaching and popular piety have surrounded the mother of Jesus in a haze of unreality. In fact she was a simple, savvy young woman who probably expected nothing in life but to be a good wife to Joseph and mother to whatever children God blessed her with in due time. In keeping with other Jews of the day, it seems she longed for Israel to be rid of the Romans and for the glory days of the past to be restored (see verses 46–55 and below). A visit from Gabriel changed both her life and the course of world history for ever.

But the story doesn't start well. Nazareth was viewed with suspicion by the Jews who lived in the south of Judea, around Jerusalem. It was full of Gentiles, and many of its Jewish residents pursued unclean trades and had too much intimate contact with outsiders. On top of that, Luke stresses that Mary was a virgin. These were two reasons that made it unlikely that anything significant would happen here. And yet it does, because God is the God of the impossible and the unlikely (verse 37).

Mary was clearly puzzled and afraid (verse 29). Not only was there an angel in her kitchen, but he greeted her with words that must have made her blush – 'highly favoured' (verse 28), 'found favour with God' (verse 30).

Gabriel's gentle command that she shouldn't be afraid (verse 30) probably has less to do with his sudden appearance – though that would have been as unsettling for Mary as it had been for Zechariah – than with the content of his message. It is hard to imagine anything that would disturb a bride-to-be more than being told she is about to become pregnant. Luke has already told us twice in verse 27 that Mary is a virgin, and Mary herself tells us the same fact in verse 34.

But her virginity is not the most staggering element of the story; the identity of her son is. He will be the king, promised long ago to David, who will sit on his throne for ever (verse 32; see 2 Samuel 7:11–16). More than that, he will be the 'Son of God'. This too was a title that had been given to Israel's kings. But clearly it means more than that here, because in response to Mary's incredulous 'How will this be?' the angel says that Jesus will be conceived by God's Spirit coming upon Mary (verse 35) and so will be holy.

The teenager's response to all this is quite amazing, albeit couched in such matter-of-fact tones. Whereas the priest Zechariah doubted and disputed with the angel, Mary simply listened and believed. More than that, she willingly co-operated with God's plan despite the obvious trouble it would cause her with her family, her village and, of course, her fiancé.

She goes off to see Elizabeth – perhaps the only person in the world who would understand what she was feeling. In Elizabeth's warm greeting, Luke is able to remind his readers of the wonder of Mary's faith. Mary is 'blessed', she says, a word known to us from the so-called 'beatitudes' (see 6:20–22; Matthew 5:3–11), meaning 'fortunate' or 'lucky', because she has believed what God said (verse 45).

The phrase echoes what was said of Abraham's faith in Genesis 15:6.

Mary's fuller response to God is contained in the song that completes this section, which we know as the *Magnificat*. The song also ties up the threads of the story so far and anticipates many of the themes yet to come in Luke's Gospel.

Two ideas dominate the song: God the warrior, routing the arrogant, and God the gentle, reaching down to help his people. He is described as the Mighty One (verse 49) who scatters enemies, defeats rulers and unseats the proud (verses 51–52). But he is also merciful to his people, lifting up the humble, feeding the hungry, remembering his promises (verses 52–54). Mary herself is an example of this grace: God is not just Israel's Saviour, he is also Mary's (verse 47); she joins the ranks of the 'lucky' (as described in Psalm 1) who are swept up into God's arms because of his faithfulness to his promises.

Mary is caught up in the fulfilment of God's promise to Abraham, his promise that he would rescue his people and through them rescue the world. Through her son, now growing in her womb, God will bring good news to the humble and hungry, but sharp words to the arrogant and rich (see, for example, 6:20ff; 12:1–34; 16:1–31; 19:1–10).

This plan, a thousand years in the making, is nearing its climax through this ordinary, Galilean peasant girl. No wonder Mary is excited and thrilled! Her song, the first of four in this opening section of the Gospel, highlights another of Luke's themes: praise. When God acts, the proper response is worship and praise, not just obedience.

Questions

1. Can you think of 'ordinary' people whom God has used to do 'extraordinary' things? Share experiences. How do such stories make you feel?
2. Do angels appear today? If so, what do they do, and why? See Hebrews 1:14.

3. Particularly if you are studying in a group, why not plan a time of worship based on Mary's song – either for yourselves or for a wider group?

The incarnation

Luke tells us a lot about who Jesus is at the beginning and end of his story. Use the following verses to create a picture of Jesus and ask whether it adds up to Luke giving us a doctrine of incarnation – that is, God becoming flesh and living among us (to pinch John's phrase in John 1:14).

What Zechariah said   1:17, 69; 1:76–79: His son would pave the way for someone who is at least a king.

What does 'Lord' mean here? (See Isaiah 40:3.)

What the angel said to   1:31–33: Jesus = Saviour; Son;
Mary   king.
1:35: conceived by the Holy Spirit; holy; God's Son.

'Son of God' was a title for Israel's kings (see Psalm 2). Is that all it means here, or is there more to the title as given by the angel to Jesus?

What angels said to   2:11: Saviour and Messiah,
shepherds   though humbly born.

What Simeon said   2:29–32: A Saviour, a light to the Gentiles, he reaches beyond Israel to the world.
4:17–21: Anointed by the Spirit, fulfilling Isaiah 61:1–12.

What Jesus said	20:41–44: More than just a king.

See 'The Son of Man', p. 191, for an assessment of what this title meant on the lips of Jesus.

The disciples' final word	24:52: Would good Jews worship a man, however exalted and amazing? I don't think so.

So, what do you think? Who is Jesus, according to Luke?

Luke 1:57–80

The messenger is born

The first of the key players arrives on the stage, just as the angel foretold – and Elizabeth and Zechariah's village is alive with wonder and questions.

 John's birth is narrated in a single verse (57). What is far more important is the name he will be given and what it signifies, which takes up the rest of this section. The rejoicing neighbours expect him to be named after his father. But both parents insist he'll be called John, the name the angel gave him, meaning 'God is gracious'.

For Elizabeth, insisting on this name is straightforward enough (verse 60) – though it has to be done in the teeth of the astonishment of friends and family alike (verse 61). It was almost unheard of not to name a male child after his father or at least a prominent member of the family. But for Zechariah, who had doubted the angel's word to him all those months ago, it is an altogether more taxing act. He has

to motion for a tablet and write the name for all to read
(verse 63). Immediately, though, his speech returns – just as
Gabriel had said (verse 20). And his first words were in
praise of the God who had heard and answered his cry for a
child and for the salvation of Israel, and graciously restored
his speech even though he'd doubted his word.

His neighbours were awestruck, and word spread
quickly through the surrounding villages (verse 65). The
key question on all their lips was, 'What then is this child
going to be?' (verse 66). We readers know, of course,
because Luke has already told us. But it is still to be
revealed to the expectant and longing people of Israel.

It is in answer to that question that Zechariah sings the
song of praise that we know as the *Benedictus* (verses 67–79).
Luke tells us that this is prophecy inspired by the Holy
Spirit (verse 67) – that is, what Zechariah is about to say is
especially important for understanding what Luke's story is
about.

Speaking in the prophetic past tense, so characteristic of
Israel's prophets (e.g. Isaiah 54:1ff.), Zechariah tells his
stunned neighbours that God has redeemed his people by
raising up a Saviour in the 'House of David' (verse 69). But
this can't be a prophecy about *his* son, because he is not
from David's house; he is a priest, not a royal prince.
Immediately his audience would be wondering all the more
what and who he is talking about.

Before revealing the answer to that question, he reminds
us that this has been a long time coming. The events
unfolding now have been long expected and are happening
because God is faithful to the covenant he swore to
Abraham (verse 73). He and Mary are singing from the
same hymn-sheet.

Fulfilling the promise to Abraham concerns the creation
of a people who will serve God in the world without fear
(verse 74) – that suggests in a land where there is no
oppression by outside forces – and in holiness and
righteousness (verse 75). This is the fulfilment of God's
promise to Abraham to create a people who would reflect
something of the character of God to the lost and searching

world and, thus, lead people back to God.

This paves the way for Zechariah to spell out the role his son, John, would have in all this. He will go before the Lord, preparing the way for him (verse 76) – words that echo Isaiah 40:3 and which will be used explicitly by Luke of John in 3:4–6.

John's message will be one of grace (as his name implies): salvation will come to God's people through the forgiveness of their sins, because God feels a 'tender mercy' towards his people (verse 78). Indeed, God wants his light of grace to shine on *all* who live in darkness (verse 79). This phrase contains a note of the universal character of God's love about to be revealed in the coming of his Son. Luke is paving the way for introducing, in the sermon at Nazareth (see on 4:14ff.), Jesus' ministry of proclaiming good news to the outsider as well as to Israel.

God's reason for revealing himself to those who are in darkness is that he might bring 'peace' (verse 79). This was the theme of the angels' song to those arch outsiders, the shepherds, who were invited to celebrate the birth of Jesus (2:14). 'Peace' recalls the Hebrew word 'shalom', which is about wholeness and well-being, a renewal of relationships with God and one another, a restoration of God's intention for his creation. What God is unleashing through the birth of a son to this elderly couple is cosmic in scope: the world will be changed as a result of his coming.

Luke rounds off the story by telling us that John grew and became strong in spirit (verse 80). By this he probably means the Holy Spirit, rather than some vague reference to developing an indomitable human spirit. He also stresses that he lived in seclusion until the time came for his public ministry to begin. This has given rise to speculation about whether John might have lived in one of the monastic communities, such as the Essenes at Qumran (see p. 136), that thrived in the Judean wilderness at this time. There is no evidence for this, however.

The stage is now set, the audience expectant for the birth of Mary's son.

Questions

1. Zechariah's song is full of 'theology' – that is, of powerful thoughts about God, his purposes and his will for his people. Modern songs tend to concentrate on our response and tend to be less 'theological'. Is this a bad thing, or just a different style?
2. When is it right to go against the opinion of others because we believe God has spoken to us?
3. 'To serve him ... in holiness and righteousness ... all our days' (verse 75). Be practical: how can we do this? What's the key?

Luke 2:1–52

The Saviour is born

Kings cause disruption in the lives of ordinary people. Jesus, the long-promised king, is no different. But his disruption brings salvation.

The key character in Luke's story is about to take the stage, and yet the author talks more about Caesar than Christ and more about the shepherds  than the Holy Family (verses 1–20). Again the full significance of what is happening comes out at the naming of the child (verses 22–40). Luke then offers an insight into Jesus' growing character (verses 41–52).

Four times Luke mentions the census that takes Joseph and Mary south from Nazareth to Bethlehem (verses 1, 2, 3, 5). The picture presented is of a world that is ruled over by an absolute power – Gaius Octavian (Augustus Caesar), adopted son and heir of Julius Caesar. He had come to his throne in 27 BC and was now openly worshipped as a son of god. The empire was well organized and efficiently run (broken down into areas each overseen by a governor such as Quirinius, verse 2). The periodic censuses of the kind Luke mentions here were to assess the number of people within the empire who could be taxed and the number of men available for military service (though the people of Israel were exempted from serving in the Roman army).

Into this ordered, compliant world comes a king even more powerful than Augustus. We know this because of Mary's song and Zechariah's prophecy. We wouldn't know it from the detail Luke supplies here: a baby born while this couple were in crowded Bethlehem, staying in a house that was bursting at the seams so that the newborn could only be placed in a downstairs feeding-trough (verses 6–7; see 'Where was Jesus born and does it matter?' p. 40).

The first visitors to Israel's new king were not palace officials or members of the Jerusalem hierarchy, but shepherds (verse 8). These were men from the margin of society – the gypsies or migrant workers of first-century Palestine. Summoned by angels (verse 9), they came to see what God was doing not just for them, not just for Israel, but for the whole world (verses 10, 11, 14). And the sign to show that something out of the ordinary was happening was that the baby would be in a manger (verses 12, 16): truly a Saviour arriving humbly, dwelling among the poor and lowly of the earth, a Saviour for shepherds – but one who would threaten the position of emperors (cf. 1:52–55).

The shepherds rejoice at what's been revealed to them (verse 20), the people are amazed (verse 18) because something new and incredible is happening here and now, but Mary quietly ponders each new event (verse 19): all these responses are surely appropriate ways of greeting the Christ-child.

After eight days, Jesus is taken to the temple in Jerusalem to be circumcised and named. Here at the heart of Israel's faith and national identity, their new king arrives incognito, unrecognized except by two faithful, elderly saints, Simeon and Anna (verses 25, 36). These two dominate the story of Jesus' presentation, just as Zechariah takes centre stage at John's naming.

Simeon, old and devout, has been awaiting the deliverance of God's people from the Romans and the coming of God's rule of justice and joy (that's the force of 'consolation' in verse 25). Twice Luke tells us that this man is inspired by the Holy Spirit (verses 25, 27), indicating that what he says about the child is vital for our understanding of who he is. Taking the infant Christ in his arms, he praises God and declares that the baby is the salvation of Israel (verse 30). But more than that – and for the first time explicitly – Simeon tells us that what's happening here is for the Gentiles as well as for Israel. No wonder Mary and Joseph are amazed (verse 33)!

And now we hear the first suggestion that the coming salvation brings a cost as well as a benefit. Simeon, speaking directly to Mary, says her son will cause many to rise and fall in Israel (verses 34–35a); that is, he will bring division among the people of God (something Jesus says of himself later, 12:51–53). More than that, it will involve a pain that only a mother can experience (verse 35b) – surely a poignant reference to the agony of the cross, as well as to the up-and-down relationship she had with her son during his ministry (cf. 8:19–21).

The significance of Anna (verses 36–38) is that she is a woman. Women in Luke's day were not taken seriously as witnesses in court. Luke spells out her credentials: great age, even greater devotion to God, never leaving the temple, fasting and praying: an example of piety many men would do well to follow. She told everyone who Jesus was. Like the shepherds, she had seen and believed and now had to tell others: this is a model of active faith that Luke will commend on countless occasions throughout his story.

The family returns north. Normal life is resumed. Jesus grows up in a godly household: every year his parents go to the temple for Passover (verse 41). No wonder he grows in wisdom and the favour of God (verse 40); he has a godly model to imitate.

On the eve of his bar mitzvah, the family attends the Passover and sets off home, unwittingly leaving Jesus behind. There's real anxiety in Mary and Joseph's search (verses 44–45), spelled out to the errant boy in verse 48. There is a pre-echo of the tomb in the 'three days' of verse 46 – as though the agony of waiting and longing, hoping and fearing of the parents' search is a taste of the bereavement to come, just as Simeon suggested.

Verses 46–47 also give a flavour of what's to come: Jesus debating with the scholars of his day and amazing people with his knowledge and wisdom. The amazement here is heightened by the relative youth of Jesus. Verse 49 gives an even stronger hint (displaying the beginnings of Jesus' self-awareness) of the enigma of his presence. His parents didn't understand why he should be in the temple when he should have been going home with them (verse 50), but Mary added this episode to the many that had gone before it, all pointing mysteriously to the wonder of her son (verse 51).

Jesus continued to grow in wisdom (verse 52), notwithstanding the fact that his wisdom had already bowled the people over (verse 47). Like John, he is preparing for the beginning of his public mission. The introduction to Luke's story is over, the characters are announced and waiting in the wings: the drama of the salvation of the world can now begin its final decisive act.

Questions

1. Compare the responses to the coming of Jesus in verses 13, 14, 18–20, 25–32 and 36. Which do you identify with? Taking your cue from verses 18–20, what's your response to the coming of Jesus?
2. Anna is a sterling example of faith to us. Think of someone you know, or know of, who sets an example. What do you learn from him or her?
3. How can we encourage the children in our church to be aware of God's call on their lives?

Where was Jesus born and does it matter?

The traditional Christmas picture of Jesus in the manger in the stable is a powerful one in the western psyche. In the Eastern Orthodox tradition, Jesus was born in a cave. Neither reflects the likely historical reality of Jesus' birthplace.

Jesus was born in Bethlehem in Judea at the time of Herod the Great, when Augustus was Caesar in Rome. He was visited by shepherds (who were invited by angels) and magi (summoned by a star). That much Luke and Matthew tell us. The rest of the story about how Jesus' birth took place that appears in nativity plays owes more to the imagination and sentimentality of the Victorians than to the New Testament.

The New Testament teacher Kenneth Bailey, who has lived most of his working life in Lebanon, was once asked by a puzzled Lebanese Christian, 'Why would Joseph, a descendant of David, in the city of his family's origin, have to seek shelter in an inn and be turned out into a stable?' His answer is summarized here.

Based on Luke 2:7 ('the inn') the traditional story is that Joseph and Mary turn up in Bethlehem, can't find any room to stay at an inn and end up in a stable, and the night they arrive, Jesus is born. This contradicts the text of Luke 2, which says that the couple went up to Bethlehem and then, 'While they were there, the time came for the baby to be born' (verse 6). Obviously, the baby was not born the night they arrived in the crowded town.

This raises the question of where they stayed: were they in a stable for weeks, a cave or a private home? Bailey suggests that Jesus was born in a private home. This conclusion is based on two things: the nature of the Palestinian extended family and the layout of the typical Palestinian home.

First, family ties. Joseph's family was from Bethlehem. It is inconceivable that he had no living relative in the town. If he did, it is equally inconceivable that he would not have sought them out and that they would not have offered hospitality.

Second, a typical Bethlehem home. The typical house consisted of a living area for the family and, at one end, set about 4ft lower than the living area, the place where the family's donkey, sheep or cow was brought in at night. Mangers were set into the 'step', where the animals could feed. Wealthier homes had a second floor (often with a guest room as in Luke 22:11), but still the ground floor was part-occupied at night by animals.

Such a house is presupposed in Matthew 5:15, for instance, where a lamp is put on a stand so it gives light to *all* who are in the house; and in Luke 13:15, where on the Sabbath people would lead their animals from the manger (in the house) to the well to drink.

But what about the inn? The Greek word *katalyma* has three meanings, 'inn', 'house' or 'guest room'. In the parable of the good Samaritan, where Luke wants to speak of a commercial inn (a rarity in first-century Palestine), he uses a different word (*pandocheion*). But there is another problem with reading 'inn' in Luke 2:7 and it is that an inn is hardly the kind of place where a woman could give birth. Such inns as there were were merely larger versions of private houses where all the guests shared one large room – hardly somewhere appropriate for a birth. One assumes the *katalyma* of Luke 2:7 was a place where a birth could have taken place – only it was full.

If it doesn't mean 'inn', how about 'house'? It is unlikely to mean that in the context, since we are told that Jesus is laid in a manger and that mangers would be inside the house.

So, it is likely that *katalyma* here means 'guest room'. This is clearly what is being referred to in Luke 22:11, where we are told about a house with a 'guest room' large enough for Jesus and his friends to eat in.

▶ What happened, then, on that first Christmas? Mary and Joseph came to Bethlehem because they had to register for tax purposes in the ancestral home of the head of the household (Joseph). They found lodgings with a relative of Joseph – a distant cousin, maybe, as Joseph and Mary lived in faraway Nazareth, probably having been born there – and shared the family room. When the night came for Mary to deliver her child, she went down with the other women of the household to the place where the animals were stabled because the guest room was occupied – perhaps by a wealthier relative or a sick one. The baby was then swaddled – a practice Palestinian and Lebanese parents still follow today – and laid in a manger (an ideal cot, warm with hay).

▶ Does it matter? Yes. The traditional Christmas story of the stable removes Jesus' birth from the everyday experience of normal people and makes it something more like a fairytale. As Bailey notes, the shepherds are told that the baby in a manger will be a sign; when they've found that, they've found the right newborn baby. 'That is, he is born in a simple peasant home with the mangers in the family room. He is one of them. With this assurance they go with haste,' he says. Jesus is truly Emmanuel, God with us (Isaiah 7:14), born in an ordinary poor home, the house visited by magi some time later (Matthew 2:11).

Luke 3:1–20

The wild man in the desert

John explodes into a world feverish with expectation, bringing a message that goads his hearers to take action or face the consequences.

 Jesus' ministry was confined to Galilee and Judea. John's was even more narrowly focused. But Luke sets both in the broadest of contexts (verse 1). Tiberius succeeded Augustus in around AD 11. So these events unfold in the late 20s. Herod the Great's murderous reign ended in 4 BC and his kingdom was divided among his sons Herod Antipas, Philip, Archelaus and Lysanias. Nine years later, the Romans brought Judea under direct rule following the rejection of Archelaus by the people (see on 19:11–27). Pontius Pilate arrived as governor around AD 26. Detailed mention of these rulers is not simply a chronological marker. Luke is telling us that the events he's about to narrate have a global reach and significance.

These power-brokers are joined by two others in verse 2: Caiaphas, the current high priest and Annas his father-in-law, the real power behind the temple hierarchy. Annas had been high priest for ten years until AD 16, but he remained the dominant figure in an oppressive structure in league with the Romans.

Recalling the angel's visit and his father's prophecy, John's ministry as the last great Old Testament prophet starts in characteristic fashion: 'the word of God came to John son of Zechariah' (verse 2).

The use of Isaiah 40:3–5 (quoted by Luke in verses 4–6) is hugely significant. These words, originally spoken to the people of Israel in exile in Babylon, announced the end of their captivity. Soon they would be going home to freedom and new life. Israel was no longer physically in exile, but because of the Roman occupation, the oppression of foreign rule, the people felt themselves to be spiritually and emotionally in exile. To such people John came, telling them to get ready, just as Isaiah had before him. No wonder the crowds flocked to hear him (verse 7, cf. 21).

His message was not as comforting as that of the prophet of Isaiah 40. No bringer of good news, he lashed his audience with a passion that Jonah would have envied (see Jonah 3:4). The reason for this is seen in his reference to Abraham (verse 8). He warns the people not to trust in their ethnic heritage. God is fulfilling his promise to Abraham (1:55) to save the world, not merely Abraham's family. The people flocking to the Jordan are under God's judgment, says John – regardless of their national identity (another reminder that they are in exile). They will not gain entrance to the coming kingdom merely because of their family ties.

John's words are an attack on a key part of a first-century Palestinian's identity. They thought that by their birth they were specially related to God, a fact reinforced by the presence of the temple in their midst, where sins were atoned for and the law kept and read. In their astonishment they plead with John to tell them what to do in order to be included in the gracious promises of the coming God contained in Isaiah 40 (verse 10).

He has already talked about producing 'good fruit' (verse 9), and 11–14 spells out what this means. What is striking is that it has precious little to do with religious observance. John does not tell them to pray more, visit the temple more frequently or lead a Bible study. Rather, he tells them to share their goods (verse 11), do their work honestly (verse 13), act justly in all their dealings with people and to be content with what they have (verse 14). This is a revolutionary message that we will find on the lips of Jesus as well: true faith in Abraham's God means living graciously out of our experience of receiving grace.

It's no surprise that the crowd thinks John is 'the Messiah' (verse 15). The picture people had of the coming

Messiah at this stage was pretty fluid. They didn't really know what to expect – hence their wondering about John. Perhaps the Messiah would be an Elijah-type prophet, perhaps a warrior king like David, perhaps a priest like Melchizedek (who had blessed Abraham, Genesis 14:18–19). Given such a wide range of options, John could be the one.

He scotched such talk emphatically by contrasting his ministry with that of one even more powerful and mysterious than he (verse 8). He says he isn't worthy to be his domestic servant (verse 16b), and stresses that he is merely the 'voice' of Isaiah 40:3, not the coming Lord. Then he contrasts his baptism (in water as a sign of repentance) with that of the coming one. He will baptize in the Holy Spirit and fire (verse 16c). These two baptisms are the twin aspects of the Messiah's ministry. The Holy Spirit signifies the new life and renewed relationship with God that the Messiah brings. John does not dwell on this. He emphasizes the fire of judgment that the Messiah will also bring. Jesus speaks of this fire in 12:49 in relation to his own impending death.

John was a fearless prophet, speaking the same uncompromising message to all and sundry – including the most powerful in the land (verse 19). For this he paid the ultimate price – but Luke rounds this section off with the forerunner of God's Messiah languishing in Herod Antipas's jail.

Questions

1. Would you have gone out into the desert to see John? Why?
2. Think about your Monday to Friday occupation, whatever it is. In all honesty, are there things for which John would call you to repent? Share them if appropriate.
3. John spoke out fearlessly against Herod, and against the soldiers' and tax collectors' exploitation of the civilian population (implied in verses 13–14). Should we do the same? When should we keep quiet?

Luke 3:21 – 4:13

Calling and testing the Saviour

**Jesus arrives quietly as part of the crowd around John.
Immediately he is the focus of the ultimate battle between
God and the forces of darkness.**

Luke is less interested in telling us about
Jesus' baptism than in emphasizing his
identity as Son of God (3:22, 38; 4:3, 9) and
his empowering with the Holy Spirit
(3:22; 4:1, 9). These two things are inextricably linked (1:35).
They form the essential backdrop to our understanding of
who Jesus is and what he has come to achieve.

The section opens with Jesus as just one of those who
came to be baptized by John (verse 21). In that humble act
he was not only identifying with the sinful multitudes
around him – something that would lead him to the cross to
die for their sins; he was also endorsing John's ministry and
especially the things that John had said about the coming
Messiah.

The focus of Luke's interest, however, is later when Jesus
is praying *after* his baptism. Withdrawing and praying was
a frequent practice of Jesus (5:16; 6:12; 9:18). In this scene of
intimacy with his Father, we read that heaven opened, the
Holy Spirit came and a voice spoke. The scene contains
echoes of Ezekiel 1:28 – 2:2 with its picture of the voice
coming along with the Spirit to empower the prostrate
prophet.

Here the veil between heaven and earth is pulled aside
and we glimpse something of the realities beyond our
workaday world. God affirms the identity of this carpenter
from Nazareth with the words 'You are my Son, whom I
love; with you I am well pleased' (verse 22). They are drawn

from Psalm 2:7 and Isaiah 42:1. Luke is telling us more than the fact that Jesus is God's Son; after all, he's told us that already (1:32, 35). He's telling us what kind of Messiah Jesus is. Psalm 2 reminds us he is a king, while Isaiah 42, the second of the four servant songs of Isaiah 40 – 55, tells us that he is the one who will bring God's salvation to the nations (not just Israel) and that he will suffer to do it (as the final song tells us: Isaiah 52:13 – 53:12).

To emphasize both Jesus' identity as Son of God and the universal nature of his ministry, Luke interrupts the flow of his story to trace his genealogy back to Adam and hence to God (verses 23–38). That 4:1 follows directly from 3:21–22 is shown by the repetition of the location for these events: the Jordan.

From the region around the river, Jesus is driven into the desert. The Holy Spirit does the driving. What is about to happen, happens because God wants it to; this is not a case of the devil ambushing Jesus unexpectedly. In Jewish teaching there is a strong emphasis on God's faithful servants being tested, not least in the story of Abraham himself (Genesis 22; cf. Hebrews 12:3–11; Luke 3:34). In the testing, God is seeking to seal and strengthen the faith of his Son, but the devil wants to undermine it. Such is the battle in all God's servants (cf. James 1:12–18).

The forty days Jesus spends in the wilderness echoes the forty years Israel spent wandering after crossing the Red Sea. Israel was God's son (Exodus 4:22), whom he led into the wilderness. But they rebelled and failed to live up to the calling to be a light to the Gentiles (cf. Isaiah 63:10). Now God's Son is here: will he similarly fail or will he succeed in being the means by which God fulfils his original promise to Abraham? The story bristles with tension.

Jesus was hungry (verse 1), so the devil dares him to use his power to satisfy his hunger (verse 2). In each of the temptations, the devil subtly challenges Jesus' identity: '*If* you are the Son of God ...', the implication being that the fact he is hungry means that Jesus can't really be God's Son after all.

The test here is to use the power that Jesus has to serve

his own ends, even legitimate ones like satisfying his own hunger, rather than God's. If Jesus does his own thing, there can be no salvation. He will turn out to be a son like Israel was – wayward and rebellious. But Jesus reminds the devil that we are nourished by more than bread, with words that come from the great document of Israel's time in the desert: Deuteronomy. People are sustained, he says, by God's word (Deuteronomy 8:3).

So the devil shifts the focus of attack. Luke has stressed that the world is ruled by Rome (2:1; 3:1). Here we see that behind Rome lurks the demonic (cf. Revelation 13, where 'the beast' stands for Roman power; 2 Corinthians 4:4). The devil, parodying God's words to Jesus from the coronation psalm (Psalm 2:7), offers Jesus all the world's kingdoms now (verses 5–6). But what he's offering doesn't belong to him; he is going way beyond any authority God may have delegated to him. Jesus rebukes him from Deuteronomy 6:13, stressing that he is going to be faithful to the true God and Lord of this world, his Father (verse 8).

Finally the scene shifts to Jerusalem (verse 9). Foreshadowing the passion, the devil invites Jesus to test out his sonship by putting God to the test – a reversal of what's actually happening here. At the same time such a show, in the place that is the foundation of Israel's identity, would prove to a sceptical public who Jesus is and have the crowds flocking to him.

Again Jesus uses Deuteronomy (6:16) to keep his mind focused on God's plan for him. In doing so, he is stressing that divine rescue can come *through* suffering and death and not just *from* it (as Peter says of Jesus in Acts 2:24–28). To be the Son of God means to walk the path laid out for him and to do the will of his Father whatever it might cost (cf. 22:42).

And so this very private battle ends with the devil withdrawing (verse 13). Jesus is strengthened by the encounter. He knows who he is and why he has come: he is ready to begin his public ministry.

Questions

1. People often trace their family tree because it gives them a sense of identity to discover who their ancestors were. Why do you think Luke includes Jesus' family tree (verses 23–38)?
2. What are the modern equivalents of Jesus' temptations? What are the positive things about being tempted for Jesus?
3. What are the secrets of overcoming temptation?

Luke 4:14–30

The Nazareth manifesto

After his lengthy introduction, this is Luke's first report on Jesus' public ministry. Already Jesus has got a reputation as a preacher. And word of this has reached his home town. Time for some explanations.

Like all good storytellers, Luke builds pace and tension into his tale. One of the underlying themes of his narrative is the simmering conflict between Jesus and the religious establishment of his day. Here it surfaces for the first time, and the battle lines are clearly drawn. Behind the conflict, as we know because of the previous story, lurks the demonic always seeking to upset God's plans and intentions.

Jesus has gone home to see his family, having been on tour in Galilee. Naturally he goes to the synagogue and takes part. Luke says this was his custom (verse 16), a phrase that probably applies both to his attendance and to his taking part in reading and teaching. Little is known of the actual structure of the synagogue service, but it seems clear that any adult male could participate if he had something to say. The leaders of the Nazareth synagogue were probably pleased to have a local rising star in their midst.

Jesus read from Isaiah 61:1–2 and then claimed that he was the fulfilment of this influential text. Three times in verse 18 the pronoun 'me' is in an emphatic position in the Greek text: Jesus succeeds in riveting everyone's attention on him (verse 20b).

Isaiah 61 is a Jubilee text. The Jubilee was the fiftieth-year cancellation of debts, freeing of slaves and return of land to its original owners spelled out in Leviticus 25. In declaring that his ministry was one of bringing good news to the poor (see 'Who are the poor?', p. 66), Jesus is taking up and applying Jubilee themes very widely. Twice the Greek word for 'release' occurs (verse 18) – the word used in Leviticus to describe what happens in the Jubilee year.

But Jesus is not merely talking about a little economic redistribution – though that is part of his message, as is clear from his encounter with Zacchaeus (19:1–10). Rather, he is highlighting the fact that through his ministry God is calling the outcasts, those on the margins of society, even those beyond the bounds of Israel to enjoy all the benefits of being his people.

And all this is happening now through him (verse 21). This is a lot to take in – after all, Jesus was only a carpenter's son (verse 22) – but the home crowd was impressed with both him and his message (verse 22a). They expected to be the beneficiaries of the blessings that Jesus was spelling out from the Isaiah reading.

But Jesus blows it by going on to suggest that the very people who treasured this Bible passage might not enjoy its fulfilment. He quotes a well-known proverb that means 'Do to your own what you've done to others' (verse 23). His home audience expect as of right to benefit from Jesus' ministry in all its aspects, especially if the people of Capernaum have enjoyed them.

But Jesus tells them not to count their chickens. In verses 25–27 he spells out that his ministry is not just for the people of Israel. It is for the whole world. The stories he refers to from the ministries of Elijah and Elisha can be found in 1 Kings 17:8–24 and 2 Kings 5:1–19. To a fiercely nationalistic people, these passages are embarrassing: God was showing favour to Gentiles (a widow from Sidon, a leper from Syria), people who didn't belong to the kingdom of Israel. So the point Jesus is making is that the people of Nazareth shouldn't expect to be blessed just because they were Jews. Something else was needed.

Jesus' townsfolk were furious. They wanted to kill him. How often this would happen through his ministry (see e.g. 6:11; John 5:18)! Jesus proclaimed the year of the Lord's favour (verse 19), but was not favourably received by his own (verse 28; cf. John 1:11). What his home crowd found unacceptable was not that Jesus might be the bringer of all the benefits he spelled out in verses 18–19, but that others, including unclean and unholy Gentiles, might also benefit from blessing they thought they had an exclusive right to.

In many ways this episode prefigures the whole of Jesus' ministry. He proclaims the kingdom of God open to any and all who would come. The people of Israel, especially the Pharisees, resent sharing benefits they believe to be uniquely theirs. So there is growing hostility that would eventually result in Jesus being killed for proclaiming that the year of the Lord's favour might actually encompass more than just the little nation of Israel.

Questions

1. Jesus' custom was not only to attend synagogue regularly, but also to take part. Why do you think he did that? What lessons are there for our church involvement?
2. The Jubilee 2000 campaign worked for the cancellation of Third World debt. Do you think that this could be an aspect of 'release for the captives' for which we should call? 'Forgive us our debts, as we also have forgiven our

debtors' is actually part of the Lord's Prayer (Matthew 6:12). Should we take it literally, as well as spiritually?
3. Jesus' ministry was to outsiders. In what ways do we feel marginalized? How do we react when people very different from ourselves come to our church?

Luke 4:31–44

The kingdom is more than words

Words and deeds came together in Jesus' ministry like the two blades of a pair of scissors, to demonstrate the coming of God's reign.

Having laid out his programme at his home synagogue and had a taste of the reaction that would eventually lead to his death, Jesus now returns to Simon's home town of Capernaum and gets an altogether more positive, if puzzled, reaction. That this is a return visit is implied by the reference to Capernaum in 4:23. Jesus had clearly already ministered here while he toured Galilee after the temptations (verses 14–15).

His ministry here in Capernaum is to the marginalized – to the demonized (verses 33–36), women (verses 38–39) and the sick (verse 40) – exactly in accordance with his manifesto laid out in Nazareth. And his authority is seen in both his words and his actions (verses 32, 36). It is clear that both need to be seen together, the one validating and giving meaning to the other. The devil had promised Jesus authority if he worshipped him rather than God. Here Jesus demonstrates that he has authority already – through the power of the Holy Spirit and his obedience to his Father (verses 1, 14, 18).

As he had done in Nazareth, Jesus went to the synagogue and taught (verse 31). His teaching caused amazement because it had 'authority' (verse 32). It is likely (as we see elsewhere, especially in the Sermon on the Mount in Matthew 5 – 7) that his authority stemmed in part from the fact that he said what *he* thought rather than constantly quoting rabbis who had preceded him. In verse 36 it is clear that the 'authority' of Jesus' teaching was confirmed in its effect. Things happened as a result of it; it was more than mere talk.

The presence of a demonized man in the synagogue is a puzzle. But Luke stresses that the spirit in this man was evil (in contrast to the Spirit in Jesus) by using a very awkward phrase, literally meaning 'a spirit of an unclean demon'. It seems that Luke wants to emphasize that the encounter between Jesus and this man was in fact an encounter between the bringer of God's kingdom and the forces of evil (see verse 13). Jesus' authority over the demon is seen not only in the confession of who Jesus is but also in the way the man is released. The curious phrase in verse 35, where the demon 'threw' the man down but didn't injure him, is a picture of the complete submission of the evil spirit to Jesus, and its powerlessness before him. At Jesus' word, the man is freed.

Clearly the demons knew exactly who Jesus was and why he'd come (verse 34). The Holy One of God (cf. 1:35) was here to destroy the forces that kept people in bondage. Luke describes both the exorcism of the demonized man and the healing of Simon's mother-in-law with similar language: rebuke (verses 35, 39) and release ('Come out of him!', verse 35, 'and [the illness] left her', verse 39). Luke is keen to emphasize that Jesus' ministry of exorcism and healing is part of his programme of bringing release that he outlined in Nazareth (verses 18–20).

The shift of scene from the synagogue to Simon's house shows that Jesus' ministry is not confined to holy places. He demonstrates his authority and power in an ordinary family home too (verse 38). After the encounter with the demonized man, the scene at Simon's house is tender, domestic and very private. Word spreads, needless to say, and by nightfall a crowd has gathered, with a welter of needs. Jesus met each one individually (verse 40c), a reminder that he has come to bring every individual an experience of release from whatever is binding him or her.

The key focus of this section, however, is not so much on the demonstration of Jesus' authority. Rather, it is on the response of people to it. Four times in these verses we are told Jesus did something and he got a response. He taught and people were amazed (verse 32). He commanded the demons and they obeyed and people were stunned, asking, 'What's happening here?' (see verse 36). He healed a sick woman and her response is to get up and serve him – a response of gratitude from someone who has received grace (verse 39). He made an impact on a town and they wanted him to stay (verse 42) – what a contrast with his home town of Nazareth (verse 29)!

Within this range of reactions is the question: who is this Jesus? We readers know because of Luke's introduction in chapters 1 and 2, and more specifically because of the story of Jesus' baptism and temptations (3:21–22; 4:1–13). The demons know (verses 34, 41), but Jesus would not let them speak because he didn't want their testimony giving rise to speculation that he may be in league with Satan (cf. 11:14–22).

The people do not know who he is: they are amazed and intrigued, but they are left to weigh his words and actions and draw their own conclusions about what they reveal about Jesus. He will tell them only why he has come – and by implication what it is that they have experienced in his words and deeds among them. He has taught them that the reign of God has come among them (verse 43). He has to tell others the same.

Questions

---

1. Look at the different responses to Jesus. Which one is closest to yours?

2. How does evil manifest itself in our lives and communities?
3. What place is there for social action – that is, practical caring for the marginalized – on the agendas of our churches? What priority should it receive – for instance, within the church's budget?

Luke 5:1–26

The cry of faith

Jesus provoked a reaction wherever he went. But merely being intrigued is not enough. He calls people to follow him, leaving their old securities behind.

Luke has already told us that Jesus provoked a reaction wherever he went – negative (4:28) and positive (4:32, 36). He's hinted at the response Jesus is looking for (4:39). Now he tells us three stories that show us people putting their faith in Jesus, and the dramatic effect that has, not only on them, but also on those around them.

At the heart of the first story (verses 1–11) is Simon's unsettling experience of Jesus' authority and power. Of course, he has already marvelled at what Jesus can do for people in need (4:38–39). Here he sees that Jesus has claims on us even when we don't think we're in need.

Jesus is teaching at the lakeside, attracting ever larger crowds (verse 1). What could be more sensible than stepping into a handy boat and moving offshore a bit so that he's not crushed in the mêlée (verse 2)? It happens to be Simon's boat, and when Jesus has finished teaching, he decides to check out the depth of Peter's grasp of what he's about.

He tells Simon how to do his job (verse 4), and in the circumstances Simon is quite polite in his reply (verse 5). It's one thing for Jesus to talk about religious things, quite another for him to get involved in secular affairs. But Jesus is keen to show Simon that his authority knows no limits. The professionals fished all night and caught nothing (verse 5); now the nets are so full they are bursting (verses 6–7).

Simon immediately sees what this means. Jesus is no run-of-the-mill teacher and healer. He is something stunningly different. Simon's only response is worship, a recognition that in Jesus' presence, he is a sinner (verses 8–9). To the trembling, hunched figure of this burly fisherman, Jesus says, 'Don't be afraid' (verse 10). Notice that Jesus doesn't say that Simon is wrong in his assessment of him. Quite the contrary: Simon is so right that he is now in a position where he can be helpful to Jesus in his mission. So he calls him to follow, and Simon gladly drops everything and goes (verse 11).

At the heart of the second story (verses 12–16) is the simple faith of someone who has nowhere else to turn and is prepared to take an immense risk to get well. Lepers were allowed no contact with the healthy. So he risks a firm rebuke in approaching Jesus. But he does so because he believes that Jesus can heal him (verse 12).

Jesus takes an even bigger risk. His first response is to reach out and touch the leper (verse 13). Immediately Jesus would have become unclean according to the purity laws, and yet he demonstrates his authority once more in that it is the leper who is cleansed by Jesus in that touch, rather than Jesus who is polluted.

Jesus sends him to the temple because the law commanded that the priest must certify departure of the leprosy before the man can return to his family and village and whatever life he had before being struck by the awful condition (see Leviticus 13 – 14). Jesus has given this man more than a cure. He's given him back his life, brought him hope. No wonder – despite Jesus' stern warning (verse 14) – that he goes off singing Jesus' praises and telling anyone who'll listen what has happened to him (verse 15). He's put his whole trust in Jesus and Jesus hasn't let him down.

At the heart of the third story (verses 17–26) is the faith of a group for their friend, and the unsettling truth it unleashed in the process. Luke tells us the Pharisees had arrived. It is their first appearance in his Gospel; they will become more prominent in the next section. What will they make of this teacher from Nazareth?

A group arrives, desperate to get their friend close enough to Jesus for him to be healed. But the crowd around the house is heaving; they can't get through. Inspired, they climb the outside stairs to the roof, tear off enough tiles to make a gap big enough for their friend's stretcher to fit through, and lower him right at the feet of Jesus (verse 19). Every eye in the room looks up – including Jesus' – and meets the expectant gaze of the group on the roof.

Seeing their faith (both the sick man's and his friend's) Jesus forgives the paralytic his sins (verse 20). Immediately the Pharisees are up in arms. The temple is where you go to get sins forgiven. You make the proper sacrifices and throw yourself on the mercy of God. Sins cannot be removed by the word of a teacher in an ordinary family home. Such talk is blasphemy (verse 21).

Jesus knew the reaction these words would get from the new elements in his audience. That's why he said them, and why Luke repeats 'forgive' four times (verses 20, 21, 23, 24a): he's stressing that this is the central issue here. To prove that he does indeed have the authority to do what, up till now, could only be done in the temple, Jesus tells the man to get up and go (verses 24–25).

This is Jesus' first use in Luke of the term 'Son of Man' (see p. 191). The phrase might just be an Aramaic idiom for 'one'. But Jesus is more likely using it as a title for himself derived from Daniel 7:13–14, the meaning of which is enigmatic now, but which will be fleshed out in Jesus' subsequent words and actions.

The crowd is filled with awe and wonder (verse 26). They know something fantastic is happening among them. Luke doesn't tell us what the Pharisees think; their silence is rather ominous.

Questions

1. 'From now on you will catch men' (verse 10). Should we catch people for Christ like a fisherman, with tackle and bait?
2. Who are the 'lepers' in your area? Who should you touch in the name of Jesus Christ?
3. Sin is the paralysis of the soul; it makes us unresponsive towards God. Turn the room where your group meets into that room where the roof was suddenly opened. Perhaps one or two in your group would be willing to act the part of the paralytic. The rest of the group can gather round them like the four friends, bringing them with faith to Jesus.

Discipleship

'**A man is a man through men.**'
>   (A Zulu proverb: I'm sure it applies to women too!)

'**I hear and I forget; I see and I remember; I do and I understand.**'
>   (A Chinese proverb)

Jesus called people to follow him (5:10b–11, 27–28) and those who followed were called 'disciples'. A disciple is someone who learns by following and imitating a master.

What does it mean to be a disciple of Jesus? Study the following verses and build up a picture of what being a disciple of Jesus involves.

Being like our teacher   6:40: Discipleship means imitating our master's lifestyle.

What 'training' does Jesus have in mind here? See 6:20–49 for clues.

Asking questions	8:9: Sometimes daft ones(!): 9:54 (cf. 52–56).
Being involved in Jesus' work	9:1–6: Going on mission. 9:10: Debrief with Jesus. 9:12–17: Feeding the 5,000. 10:1–17: Going on mission. 10:18–24: Debrief.

When should we be encouraging new disciples to go on mission? What was Jesus' practice?

Bearing the cost	9:57–62; 14:26–33; 18:18–29.

Are we prepared to surrender everything to follow Jesus? What does this mean in practice?

Failure	9:38–40: Failure in ministry. 22:43: Failure in prayer.

Are we prepared to learn the hard lessons of failing?

Luke 5:27 – 6:16

Refounding Israel

As Jesus fleshes out his programme, it propels him into ever more direct conflict with the leaders of Israel. Only one course of action is open to him.

It now becomes clear what the Pharisees were thinking at the end of the last section. Here Jesus clashes head-on with them over who is

included in God's people. He scandalizes the Pharisees by paying scant attention to the rules and rituals that ordered the life of a good first-century Jew. The four incidents in this section – relating to mixing with 'sinners', eating with the unclean and flouting the Sabbath, show that Jesus' mission to bring good news to the poor impacts everyone. It climaxes with the Pharisees plotting Jesus' downfall (6:11), and Jesus refounding Israel (6:12–16). Which will win out in the end – their old Israel, with its old 'wineskins' of strict rules and regulations, or his new one?

In a sense the calling of Levi is just another example of Jesus calling people to follow him (verse 27). In reality it's far more than that. Tax collectors were loathed by the people and seen as unholy by the Pharisees. They lived by putting a bid into Rome to collect the tolls for a region, paying the money up front and then collecting the taxes plus whatever 'expenses' they saw fit to add.

Levi's response is immediate (verse 28). Clearly, 'leaving everything' does not mean that he walked away from his possessions and money, otherwise he could not have thrown the banquet (verse 29). Rather it's Luke's way of telling us that he left one way of life and took up a new way of living as a disciple of Jesus, which included putting all his possessions at Jesus' disposal. In other words, his repentance affected not just his religious observance but his whole lifestyle (cf. verse 32).

Jesus doesn't just mix with tax collectors and their friends; he eats with them (verse 29). Table fellowship was a sign of acceptance. Notice the Pharisees call the 'others' at the banquet (verse 29) 'sinners' (verse 30). It is their way of declaring that these people are excluded from God's kingdom. Eating with them is Jesus' way of declaring that they are included.

He spells this out by talking of his mission in terms of calling all people, Pharisees included, to repentance (verse 32) and a new way of living (which he will spell out in detail in 6:17ff.). The Pharisees are keen to show that they are already righteous by changing the subject to fasting. They contrast the behaviour of their disciples (and those of the still-popular John) with that of Jesus' followers (verse 33). Clearly they are attacking Jesus himself.

The underlying issue here is: who is part of Israel? Rules about table fellowship and fasting, as well as keeping the Sabbath (6:1–11), were ways of drawing boundaries around the 'in' crowd. The Pharisees felt themselves to be 'in' and those who did not behave like them to be 'out'. Jesus is redrawing the boundaries to include those excluded by such rules, saying that repentance is what determines whether one is included in God's people or not.

The Old Testament uses the picture of marriage to describe God's relationship with Israel (e.g. Hosea 2:14–23; Ezekiel 16; Isaiah 54:5–6; 62:4–5). Jesus makes the same claim for himself (verse 34). He goes on to explain this with a parable which suggests that the new thing he is doing, which is the fulfilment of God's original plan, starting with Abraham (cf. 1:55; 2:30–32), cannot be contained in the structures that have grown up around the Pharisees. They are too restrictive. They exclude too many people (verses 36–37). Of course, the Pharisees find them very comfortable and aren't likely to give them up (verse 39).

With chapter 6 the scene shifts to two separate incidents on two different Sabbath days. The underlying issue is the same, however, and this gives this section its unity. The fact that many days or weeks separate each of these events shows that the controversy between Jesus and the Pharisees grew over a period of time, and was not based on a single incident which could have been a misunderstanding.

The Sabbath (Saturday) was the day of rest in Israel, the day when, according to the law, the people remembered how God rescued them from slavery in Egypt and set them free. By the time of Jesus, the Sabbath had become another boundary that separated pious Jews from 'sinners'. Not surprisingly, Jesus had something to say about that.

The two Sabbath disputes, however, are less about the nature of the day itself and more about who has authority to determine what happens on the Sabbath. The Pharisees claimed, on the basis that they were custodians of the traditions of Moses, that they had the right to legislate for what people did on the Sabbath. This was another way they could control who was 'in' and who was 'out'.

Jesus didn't agree. The first story has to do with who has authority to interpret the law. The example from the life of David (see 1 Samuel 21:1–7; 22:9–10) concerns David and his men doing something the law forbade (Exodus 25:30; 39:36; 40:22–23; Leviticus 24:5–9). It's an example of the letter of the law being set aside to prevent the spirit of the law being flouted – namely that hungry people should be fed. Jesus uses the story to claim that he has the right to interpret the law and so to determine behaviour acceptable on the Sabbath (verse 5).

The second episode concerns a healing which didn't have to happen there and then. The man's life was not in danger. His hand would still be shrivelled tomorrow; Jesus could heal it then. That he chooses to do it now means that he is making a point about his authority to say what should and shouldn't happen on the Sabbath (verse 9). Do we use the law to restrict and exclude, or do we live by it to bring to others the freedom we enjoy because of it? What comes first, the niceties of strict doctrine, or the need of the people? Jesus chooses the latter – the healing being proof of his authority over the Sabbath.

The Pharisees now know that the only way to retain their position is to get rid of Jesus (verse 11). Jesus knows that he must flesh out the implications of his teachings and activity by refounding Israel (verses 12–16). After a night of prayer (verse 12), he gathers his disciples and from their number selects twelve (after the twelve tribes of Israel) to be called 'apostles' (meaning 'authorized representatives'; verse 13). In view of the failure of Israel's current leadership to live up to God's calling to be a light to those in need in Israel (and beyond), Jesus creates a new leadership. That it is largely symbolic is clear from the fact that most of those named play no further significant role in Luke's story.

What is it symbolic of? It shows that Jesus is refounding God's people on the basis of how individuals, whatever their background, respond to his presence among them. Repentance is the key to being 'in' the people of God.

Questions

1. Do you have comfort zones that are challenged by the new wine of Jesus' message? What are they?
2. Would Jesus have joined the Keep Sunday Special campaign? Why or why not? (This campaign has sought to restrict Sunday trading by shops and businesses in Britain.)
3. 'Not the niceties of strict doctrine, but the needs of the people.' Would Jesus make this a manifesto for the church of the twenty-first century? What might this mean in practice?

Luke 6:17–49

The lifestyle of the kingdom

Jesus appeared to sweep away the old rules concerning table fellowship, fasting and Sabbath-keeping. So how should his followers live?

The Pharisees could well have accused Jesus of turning religion into a free-for-all. Paul was accused of much the same later (see e.g. Romans 6:1ff.; Galatians 5, especially verses 16ff.). If you did away with all the rules the Pharisees so rigorously applied, what were you left with? For Jesus, lifestyle grows out of the heart, not the rule book. It starts with a recognition that we're not holy, good and pure (verses 20–23), but stand in need of God's grace. Then, having freely received from him, we live like him towards others (see the key verses 35b–36, 40 and 45c).

The crowds are getting bigger – not just from Galilee but

from the coastal areas (Tyre and Sidon) and the south (Judea). Jesus' reputation is growing. They've come to be healed (verses 18–19). But Jesus is keener to teach those who really want to know what he's about (his disciples, verse 20). Like the Sermon on the Mount (Matthew 5 – 7), this so-called 'Sermon on the Plain' is either a collection of Jesus' sayings which the author has brought together, or the report of an actual sermon Jesus gave. If the latter, it is not the same one Matthew records.

But it starts the same way – probably indicating that this was something Jesus said frequently – with a series of 'beatitudes'. 'Blessed' means 'happy' or 'lucky'. It had a long history in Israel as the word used to describe those who stood in a right relationship with God (e.g. Psalm 1). In keeping with his Nazareth manifesto (4:17–21), it is the poor, the hungry, the weeping and the hated who are lucky (verses 20–23; see 'Who are the poor?', p. 66). Such people know they have nothing with which to impress God or other people. They can be included among God's people only by an act of grace on God's part, an act which he is very willing to perform (verses 20c, 21b, 21d, 23a).

The rich, full, laughing and popular, however, are not so lucky (verses 24–26). These are the ones who think that their place in God's affections is secure and they are somewhat smug about it (cf. 18:9–12). Jesus probably has the Pharisees in mind. But his words embrace all who think their status, wealth and position are signs of blessing from on high. Unless they repent, says Jesus, they have only trouble to look forward to (verses 25b, 25d).

Jesus' disciples don't have it easy, however. The lifestyle he calls them to is hard and will provoke opposition (verses 22–23). Jesus' ethic is an ethic of grace, not rules; as we have been treated by God, so we treat others. It's a tall order!

First he calls us to love our enemies. This is the opposite of the ethic of the Pharisees or the Essenes or any of the other sects and parties in first-century Israel (see 'Sects and parties', p. 135). As we saw in the last section, these parties divided the world into 'us' and 'them' and looked after their own (see on 10:25–37). Jesus says we should be like God (verses 35b–36) and be gracious to all, friend and enemy alike. The crowd must have loved the irony of the Pharisees' ethic being likened to that of the 'sinner' (verses 32–33)!

Next he calls us not to be judgmental in our attitudes towards others (verses 37–38). We should be forgiving and generous because that is God's attitude to us; indeed, our forgiveness and experience of blessing are dependent on our forgiving others and being gracious to them (verse 38b). Again, he stresses that when we have learned this, we will be like him (verse 40), and he illustrates it with one of his funniest parables (verses 41–42). The thought of trying to dab a speck of dust out of someone's eye when there is a huge log in your own is hilarious; the picture he paints is of you knocking your friend senseless as you try to help her. But as the laughing dies, the penny drops.

In verses 43–45 he reaches the heart of the matter – literally. How can we love our enemies and be forgiving and gracious? By *being* good. Such behaviour flows out of a good heart, says Jesus. (Note the threefold repetition of 'good' and 'evil' in verse 45.) It's not about learning and obeying a set of rules. It's about being changed on the inside and that change spilling out in the way we speak and behave. Such teaching anticipates Paul's emphasis on living by the Spirit in Galatians 5.

For Jesus, this happens as we listen to his word, take it into our hearts and live it out (verse 46). There were lots in his audience who thought him interesting, novel, 'flavour of the moment'. But Jesus is concerned that we shouldn't only hear his words, but do them as well (verse 47). If we take Jesus at his word and do as he says, when the trouble comes we'll be able to take it. Hearing and not doing is like building a house on sand. When the going gets tough, as it surely will if we live by Jesus' ethic, we crumble and give up (verses 48–49).

The flood (verse 48) and the torrent (verse 49) probably have a double meaning. The words refer to the immediate difficulties that arise in the world as we live as disciples of Jesus (see verses 22–23). But they also refer to the coming day of judgment. Only those who have built their lives and their lifestyles on Jesus' words will stand on that day. The others will be swept away. It is a sombre note that Jesus ends on.

Questions

1. What's so 'lucky' about being poor, hungry, sad and hated?
2. How does the call to love our enemies relate to situations such as those in Northern Ireland, the Balkans, Rwanda, or whatever ethnic or racial division is currently splashing bloody headlines around the world?
3. What are the overflowing blessings of not judging or condemning others, but instead giving and forgiving (verses 37–38)?

Who are the poor?

When we read any part of the Bible, there is a danger of reading our culture, our way of seeing the world, back into the story we are looking at. This is especially true when trying to answer the question 'Who are the poor?' in Luke's Gospel.

Two answers to this question have been offered. Traditionally, people have interpreted 'poor' to mean 'poor in spirit' (Matthew 5:3), that is to say 'humble'. More recently, people have suggested that the word should be taken at its contemporary face value and interpreted to mean those who are economically not very well off.

But both these understandings are insufficiently rooted in the culture of first-century Palestine. The term 'poor' is one of a number of words that refer not to people's economic class, material well-being or spiritual state, but to their status in the community.

Recent studies have shown that status was a crucial indicator of social position and acceptance by the community in which one lived in the ancient world. Status was something people were born with (so-called 'ascribed status') or else achieved through their own efforts (so-called 'performance status'). Ascribed status had to do with one's family, sex and genetic attributes. Performance status had to do with one's education or devotion to codes of religious or social behaviour.

▶ Priests in first-century Palestine had a wholly ascribed status. Priesthood was something you were born into; but even if you came from the right family, genetic abnormalities (such as being blind or disabled) disqualified you from the role, whatever your educational achievements. The attributes required were laid down in Leviticus 21:16–24.

▶ Joining the famous Dead Sea community at Qumran was based on both performance and ascription. You had to pass a series of probationary tests to check out whether you were a fit member of the community. But you also had to meet certain ascribed criteria: for instance, you had to be Israelite by birth and free from genetic defect. Indeed, as far as these Essenes were concerned, the disabled could not be part of the people of God.

▶ The Pharisees included and excluded people (that is, they offered or refused status) on the basis of a set of performance criteria: devotion to a certain way of reading the law of Moses, and commitment to rituals that went beyond the letter of that law, such as weekly fasting and elaborate washing before every meal.

So when Jesus says that he has come to preach good news to the poor (4:18) and that the poor are particularly 'lucky' (blessed) (6:20), it has to be understood against this background.

Just like the Essenes and the priestly authorities, Luke includes lists of defects in his Gospel. But these lists have exactly the opposite function as far as Jesus is concerned: they are intended not to exclude but to include. So Luke 4:18 lists the poor, captive, blind, oppressed; 6:20 the poor, hungry, mournful, persecuted; 7:22 the blind, lame, leper, deaf, dead and poor; and 14:13 the poor, the maimed, the lame and the blind. All these ascriptions would exclude people from Essene or Pharisaic circles. Luke's point is that these are the very people included in Jesus' circle.

Because it comes as part of Jesus' answer to the messengers sent by John, 7:22 is a key text here. John is worried that maybe Jesus isn't the one after all. Jesus reassures him by reiterating his programme statement (recorded in 4:18–19). The term 'the poor' comes at the end of the list in an emphatic place in the Greek sentence, thus demonstrating that it is a catch-all phrase that includes all the other ascriptions.

So the poor in Luke's Gospel are those on the margins of society, those left on the edge of the community, disregarded by the elite, excluded by the religious, but loved by God and special recipients of his grace. And furthermore, the elite of first-century Palestine – the Pharisees and scribes, the Sadducees and Essenes – can enjoy the benefits of God's grace only if they accept the right of these outcasts to be included and to come in the same way: with empty hands, bringing nothing. In God's kingdom the Pharisee and the lame beggar are on the same level – the latter's.

Jesus and the outsider

Jesus was prepared to take great risks to bring the good news of the kingdom to some unlikely recipients.

Both stories in this section (which continues to illustrate that Jesus' mission was the fulfilment of Isaiah 61, as he had said in the synagogue at Nazareth) show the lengths Jesus was prepared to go to in order to bring the good news to the poor.

The first story (verses 1–7) reminds us of how complex relationships were in first-century Israel. Here is a Gentile soldier, an officer in Caesar's army, the army of occupation. Truly, here is an enemy to love (cf. 6:27)! Yet he is a good man, held in high honour by the people of Capernaum where he is based (verses 4b–5), someone who is attracted to Jewish monotheism (like Cornelius, see Acts 10). The fact that the elders, the town's leaders, came to Jesus with the request for healing shows that despite Pharisaic hostility, many in Israel's elite viewed Jesus positively.

The centurion was obviously wealthy. Not only did he have servants, but he had also invested his own money in helping the town to build its synagogue. Such activity was not unheard of. Many synagogues owed their existence to Roman money: the occupying army reasoned that grateful Jews, able to worship, were less likely to revolt. We don't know whether the sick servant was a Jew or a Gentile, but it is likely that he was the latter.

The Gentile soldier sends intermediaries to the Jewish teacher (verse 3). This shows an awareness of the sensitivity felt by pious Jews about contact with Gentiles. Jesus accepts the invitation to go to the centurion's house, however. By entering the house, he risked being made ritually impure. That he was willing to go shows the radical nature of his ministry: though rich, the centurion was an outsider who needed to hear the good news that God had promised through Abraham to the world.

A second group is dispatched when Jesus hoves into view. Perhaps the centurion is alive to the difficulty Jesus might face entering a Gentile household. The message he sends amazes Jesus (verse 9). Like Peter earlier (5:8–9), this wealthy, pious man felt unworthy to be in Jesus' presence. But he recognized Jesus' absolute authority in his description of the chain of command he operated. He had only to say the word and things would happen nearby and far away from him. Surely, the centurion reasoned, Jesus' authority must be similar – only greater.

It is this that Jesus marvelled at. What a contrast with Israel! This outsider has recognized in Jesus what his own people (especially its leaders) had failed to grasp: that Jesus came with all the authority of God to bring the good news of the kingdom. And in accordance with the centurion's faith, his servant is healed.

This story raises the question: just how far does Jesus' authority extend? It is this question that links this incident with the one that follows it. It occurs in an out-of-the-way village called Nain. This is the only time this place, some 6 miles south-east of Nazareth, is mentioned in the Bible.

In the briefest of accounts, Luke presents the most extraordinary scene. Jesus is on his travels. It is almost certain that he is being followed by a crowd of disciples and assorted hangers-on. No doubt Jesus had been healing and teaching, and there would have a buzz of excitement, even a carnival atmosphere, surrounding this large group.

On the outskirts of the town, they meet another procession. At the centre of this one is the corpse of the only son of a widow. Mourners, their clothes torn, their voices raised in lament, follow on. The pain of the event is probably fresh. It is likely that the boy is being buried the day he died; this was the custom.

So Luke depicts a procession of joyous life meeting a

procession of grieving death on the edge of nowhere.

Luke describes Jesus here as 'the Lord' (verse 13), a title he uses frequently, but which here, following the incident with the centurion, reminds us of Jesus' authority. As soon as he sees the situation, Jesus is moved with pity (verse 13) and reaches out to the plank on which the corpse lies (verse 14; the NIV's 'coffin' is not really helpful).

This act instantly renders Jesus unclean (Numbers 19:11, 16). What he then says could have made him an embarrassing laughing-stock (verse 14b). But the lifeless corpse is restored to life and Jesus gives him back to his mother (verse 15). What a tender image that is!

Little wonder the crowd is awestruck. In verse 9 it's Jesus who is amazed at a Gentile's faith. Here a crowd of Jews is stunned at the authority of Jesus; he even has power over death. Do they think Jesus is the Messiah? The phrase 'great prophet' (verse 16) might suggest this. But it is more likely that they think Jesus is the greatest healer, teacher and prophet they've encountered – and they praise God for him, and his fame spreads.

Word even reaches John the Baptist in prison.

Questions

1. What was it about the centurion's faith that caused Jesus to marvel?
2. When was the last time you were 'awestruck' by something God did?
3. What does the story of the widow's son symbolize and teach? How could you turn this story into a dramatic presentation for use in worship?

Luke 7:18–50

Jesus and John: expectations and outcomes

Often what we hope for comes in a way we're not expecting. Jesus gives John, a Pharisee – and us – lessons in trusting God to fulfil his promises in his way.

While Jesus has been touring relentlessly in Galilee, John has been languishing in jail. Facing certain death, he's racked with doubt: is Jesus the one?
He'd expected to be succeeded by a judge (3:9, 16–17), so he had urged the people to be ready (3:4–6, 18). His manner and message had made the crowd wonder if he himself was the Messiah (3:15).

John has to know if he's right about Jesus. Luke tells us twice (verses 19, 20b) how desperate he is to be sure. Jesus responds by both doing (verse 21) and speaking (verses 22–23). Tell John what you see, he says; his actions, of course, are the outworking of his manifesto at Nazareth (4:18–21).

Once the messengers have departed, Jesus asks the crowd about John. Who is he? His questions in verses 24–26a are goading the crowd into thinking about their response to John's ministry. Many of them would have been baptized by John. Why? asks Jesus.

Jesus then gives his assessment of John (verses 26b–28). He is the last of the prophets who looked forward to the coming of God's reign. And he is the greatest because he heralds the arrival of that reign (verse 27b; Malachi 3:1). But those who have heard Jesus and responded by believing his message are more blessed than John because they are the first of those who can experience God's reign on earth bursting in through Jesus' ministry (verse 28).

In order to explain this, and to make sure his readers

have got the point of what Jesus is saying, Luke interjects his own comment at this point; something he rarely does (in the NIV, verses 29–30 are appropriately in brackets). John has pointed to Jesus, says Luke, and the people who'd responded to John are now responding to Jesus. Those who have been doubtful about John, namely the scribes and Pharisees, are equally doubtful about Jesus. But we mustn't write the Pharisees off; Jesus hadn't, as verses 36ff. show.

In verse 31 Luke returns to Jesus' remarks about John's ministry and his. The two are very different. He quotes a well-known proverb and likens his listeners to bored kids who can't make up their mind what they want, whether to play at weddings or at funerals (verses 31–32). John the Baptist was the rigid ascetic, and some thought him crazy; Jesus is the relaxed partygoer, and some think he's a sinner (verses 33–34). While his remarks are heard by everyone, his target here is the Pharisees who rejected John and are in danger of rejecting Jesus too – for the opposite reason.

The key verse in the section, verse 35, is a tease. Jesus is asking his hearers: 'Do you think I'm right?' A lot hangs on our response.

Immediately Jesus is invited to a party (verse 36). But his host is a prominent Pharisee – some irony in the light of verse 34! The action takes place in Nain still, scene of the raising of the widow's son and the debate about John. So the subject here is still the same. Is Jesus a prophet? Who are experiencing the reign of God in their lives?

The story of this party, with its parable at the centre, is one of Luke's most brilliant compositions, full of wit and telling observation. The contrast between the Pharisee and the woman who'd lived a sinful life is wonderfully drawn. And the end is a real cliff-hanger.

Settling at dinner, reclining at low tables with their feet out behind them, away from the table, Jesus and the other guests converse while people from the town come and go, keen to get a look at who Simon has for dinner tonight. Among them is a woman (verse 37), who creeps in and stands at Jesus' feet weeping (verse 38). Apparently she has no shame: she lets her hair down in the presence of men (something that was definitely taboo); and she showers Jesus' feet with kisses and perfume in a public display of affection that breaks all the rules of decorum.

Simon smugly assumes that this display exposes Jesus as a fraud (verse 39). Naturally, Jesus knows what he is thinking (verse 40), and in keeping with his common practice, he tells a parable (verses 41–42). It is so simple and direct that even Simon gets the point of it (verse 43)! Jesus then puts the knife directly into his host: Simon had observed none of the common courtesies associated with receiving guests (verses 44–46); no water to wash off the dust, no kiss of greeting, no oil that indicated the host esteemed his guest highly. It becomes clear that Simon has precious little respect for this carpenter from Nazareth.

The woman, however, whom we may infer had already met Jesus, spoken with him and responded to his message, showed her love for Jesus by her public display. So she was forgiven (verse 47). Yes, she was a sinner, a bigger sinner than Simon, but she'd put her faith in Jesus and so now basked in the reign of God in her life – which included the forgiveness of sins.

The other guests are up in arms at Jesus' words (verse 49). But Simon is silent. Perhaps verse 47b has made him smart a little. The encounter has certainly given him much to think about. Was this friend of sinners (verse 34) the key to the purposes of God (verse 29) that the woman found him to be? We don't know how Simon answered that question. But it's the same question we have to answer.

Questions

1. Luke presents us with a picture of boredom, or even indecision, in verses 31ff. Does it speak about people in your neighbourhood or the rest of society, perhaps? What can you say to point them to Jesus?
2. Are you comfortable with the fact that Jesus spent so much time at parties and social gatherings (compared to the amount of time he spent in church)?

3. Put yourself in the shoes first of the woman and then of Simon. What are you thinking and feeling? How do you respond as Jesus tells his parable?

Luke 8:1–21

Listening to the story of the kingdom

We'll not get the hang of Jesus unless we listen carefully to what he says and weigh his words carefully. This well-known parable has a lesson for each one of us.

The very familiarity of the parable of the sower (verses 5–8) often means we don't hear it clearly. We think we know what it's about, so we switch off. We need to read it afresh in the context in which Luke sets it. The previous section (7:18–50) dealt with our expectations about how God will fulfil his word. Now Jesus addresses the key issue of listening intently to what he is saying, and doing what he says. Luke rounds the section off by stressing that this applies to everyone, even Jesus' own mother and family (verses 19–21).

The section opens with a portrait of Jesus' travelling arrangements. Luke emphasizes that he talks about the kingdom (verse 1) everywhere he goes. And he goes on to show that the group gathering around Jesus is made up of the very people he said he'd come to gather (see 4:18–21). It contains not only the twelve – a motley assortment of working men, tax gatherers, political dreamers and fire-brands – but women. Women were among 'the poor' in Palestinian society because they had few rights. Certainly no religious teacher took them seriously; generally speaking, they weren't taught the law. These women, from every social stratum (verses 2–3a), weren't just followers; they were supporters in the full sense of the word, putting their money where their mouths were (verse 3b).

Luke indicates the numbers around Jesus in a sort of spiral: the twelve, then the women, then the crowds from many towns (verse 4). This famous parable has a big and assorted audience, which, given its subject matter, is entirely appropriate.

It is a short, complex parable which is really about three things. It's a story about Israel, about Jesus and about us. We miss the point unless we get the whole picture.

The parable retells Israel's history, a sorry tale of not listening, hardening of hearts, exile and only partial restoration (the country is still occupied by the Romans). God does not appear to be dwelling among them, and the nations are not flocking to Jerusalem to receive the law – both of which were prophesied by Isaiah about the coming kingdom. Three things point to this.

First, the parable is almost identical in structure to passages in Jewish apocalyptic (highly symbolic) writing which retell the story of Israel's relationship with God. (See, for instance, Daniel 2:31–45, which has the same fourfold structure as the sower and narrates Israel's relationship with successive world powers; see 'The kingdom of God', p. 115).

Secondly, it speaks of the 'seed', which, by the first century, had become a picture of the faithful remnant of Israel awaiting return from exile. This is why, when explaining his use of parables, Jesus quotes from Isaiah 6 (verse 10), where the prophet is told that through judgment lies redemption for the faithful few – a common apocalyptic theme (see Isaiah 6:9–13).

Thirdly, it has striking similarities with the parable of the wicked tenants (20:9–19), which is much more obviously about Israel's history. The sower is more cryptic because at this stage in his ministry Jesus cannot afford to be so open. His story is political dynamite, and Herod Antipas would silence him as he has John.

The parable is also a story about Jesus and his ministry. He has come to announce the reign of God to a people who are in exile in their own land, under Roman rule, awaiting freedom. Behind the parable lies Isaiah 55:10–13 with its promise that God's word will accomplish what it sets out to do. In that context, God had promised that the people would return from Babylon. In the sower, Jesus is saying that he is the one who is bringing the deeper fulfilment of God's plans. He is God visiting and restoring his people, bringing his reign to those who languish under foreign domination (hence the summary of Jesus' message in verse 1 as the good news of the kingdom and the need for response called for in verses 8b, 19–21).

But the parable is also a story about Jesus' listeners. This whole section is about listening and acting on what we hear. Parables intrigue or irritate, draw people in or repel them (verses 8, 16–18). Some hear and turn away. They are like the path, the rocky ground or the thorny soil. They hear, but the word washes over them like water off a duck's back. This, says Jesus, is Isaiah 6:9–10 in action. Other things are more important to these hearers than the message (verses 13–14).

Some, however, hear and want to know more. The disciples are examples of this (verse 9). And because they want it, they'll be given understanding (verse 10). There is nothing secret about Jesus' ministry; it happens in the open, not behind closed doors (verse 17). But if you want to understand what it's about, you've got to hang around, ask questions and think about it (verse 18).

But as with John, so with us, understanding comes through the eyes as well as the ears. John's messengers were told to look at what Jesus was doing (7:22), and so are we (verse 16). As well as speaking, Jesus also does things (as Luke reminds us in verse 2). Jesus is saying, 'Come and see what I've done in people's lives; come and hear what it means.'

Listening and looking, though vital, are just the prelude to living. The whole point of the parable is that the hearers will be fruitful (verses 8, 15), which is explained in terms of hearing and doing Jesus' word (verses 19–21). For this reason, Jesus' hearers are all the soils simultaneously. All of us are easily distracted, shallow and beset with the cares of the world. But all of us are potentially the rich soil in which the seed can germinate and grow into a good crop.

Questions

1. How can we *display* Jesus in our neighbourhood or town, so that people around 'see' him, and then want to hear him?
2. Jesus turns away from family life (verses 20–21) in favour of his new family (verses 1–3). Is this a pattern for us to imitate?
3. If the parable is a picture of Israel, divided between Jesus' disciples who respond to his word, and the rest who reject it, what should we conclude about the Jews today?

Parables

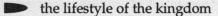

Perhaps the most distinctive feature of Jesus' teaching is his use of parables. It wasn't unique to him. Parables are found in the Old Testament and among the writings of the rabbis. But Jesus seems to have delighted in using the form to instruct the crowds. Why?

Read the following parables (all but one of which are unique to Luke) and ask yourself what they tell you about

▶ God

▶ the world we live in

▶ the lifestyle of the kingdom

▶ who Jesus is.

If you are doing this in a group, why not divide into

pairs, each of which can study one parable before presenting its findings to the rest?

8:4–8, 11–15	The sower
10:25–37	The good Samaritan
12:13–21	The rich fool
14:15–24	The great banquet
15:1–32	The lost sheep, coins, son
16:1–9	The unjust steward

In 8:9–10 Jesus tells his disciples why he uses parables. What do you make of his explanation? How do you think parables work?

Try composing modern parables to make the same points Jesus makes in the parables above.

Luke 8:22–39

Calming storms

The disciples had been let in on the secret of the kingdom of God. But they still had a lot to learn. Following Jesus can be a bit of roller-coaster ride at times.

Fear seems to have been as common a reaction to Jesus' presence as faith. It is fear that binds the two parts of this section together – the fear of the disciples (verse 25) and the fear of the people (verse 37). But not only fear. In both parts Jesus faces and overcomes malign and threatening forces (verses 23–24, 17–28). And in both the outcome of Jesus' struggle is peace (verses 24c, 35b).

Luke doesn't tell us why Jesus wants to cross the lake

(verse 22). We can infer that he wants to preach on the other side (see 8:1). His destination is Gentile territory – Jesus' only trip outside Israel. Halfway across, a storm blows up, so fierce that even experienced sailors like Peter, James and John fear they are going to drown (verse 24).

Jesus, however, must have been very tired, for he sleeps through the crisis until awakened by his fearful disciples. Jesus' quiet confidence in God is the same as that of the psalmist, who, in the midst of grave danger, is able to sleep (Psalms 3:5–6; 4:8). The disciples, however, in the first testing time they've faced since the teaching about the seed and the sower (8:12–14), find their faith has deserted them. 'Where is it?' Jesus asks once the alarm has passed (cf. verse 25). In that question is a gentle rebuke to those who've heard his teaching, been let in on the secret of the kingdom of God (8:10), and yet still have so much to learn. That rebuke will be thrown into sharper relief when the disciples' shaky faith is contrasted with that of the demonized man after he's been delivered (verses 38–39).

The disciples' fear for their lives becomes an awestruck amazement at the power and authority of Jesus (verse 25b). He commands the wind and waves (pictures in the Old Testament of the forces of chaos that only God could control) and they obey him. 'Who is this?' they ask, bewildered, scared and relieved to be in the boat with one so powerful. Again, the irony at the end is that the demonized man seems to have a clearer grasp of who Jesus is after his brief encounter with him than these disciples have, for all their time sitting at the master's feet (see verse 39, where he equates God and Jesus).

The disciples are still flummoxed when they land and are immediately confronted by another storm; this one in the form of a man besieged by demons (verse 27). So battered by the forces of evil and chaos was this nameless man that he was naked, lived among the tombs and ranted and raved like a madman who could not be controlled (verses 27, 29). He would have struck fear into most people.

But not Jesus. This is the longest exorcism recorded in the Gospels, and it is clear that it is a 'power encounter' of great proportions. Yet from the way the story is structured, we know that Jesus will come out on top. Luke tells us that the man fell at Jesus' feet and cried out in recognition of him (verse 28) before he tells us that Jesus had commanded the demon to leave him (verse 29). 'Son of the Most High God' as a title for Jesus makes sense in a Gentile context, but it is also the title Gabriel used of him in 1:32 (cf. 1:35). Interestingly, it is the same term used in the parallel story in Acts 16:16–21.

Luke then explains the nature of this man's condition to pave the way for Jesus' asking the demon's name (verse 30). A legion (verse 30) was a troop of 5,600 men: here Jesus is pitched against a whole army, but an army already trying to negotiate terms with the victor (verse 31). 'The abyss' refers to the place of destruction to which all the forces ranged against God would be consigned after the judgment.

The demons beg to go into a herd of pigs (verse 32) – the clearest evidence of all that this action takes place in Gentile territory. (Pigs were unclean animals, never kept by Jews.) Jesus grants permission and, once invaded, the pigs hurtle down the hillside to a watery grave (verse 33). The terrified herdsmen flee (verse 34), only to return with a heavy mob from the town, who are equally unsettled by what they see and hear from the herdsmen (verse 37). In their fear they ask Jesus to leave (verse 37).

Why? It's probable that Jesus had allowed the demons to enter the pigs to show everyone watching the cost to the community of healing the demonized man. What happened to the pigs could have happened to him. And while his fellow-countrymen were quite prepared to chain him up when necessary (verse 29), they weren't prepared to do anything practical to help him. Their lives went on undisturbed. Jesus heals him and rebukes the hard hearts of the townspeople through causing the pigs to be lost.

Jesus had come like a whirlwind and turned their lives upside down. The demonized man was healed, clothed, in his right mind, under control and sitting at Jesus' feet; the town's economic routine had been disrupted. It was too much for these people to take. Their fear led them to push

Jesus away, in contrast to the disciples' fear which urged them to get to know Jesus better (verses 37, 25; cf. 5:8–11).

The healed man wanted to go with Jesus. He is the first who has asked to be a disciple; all the others were there because Jesus called them to follow him. But Jesus refuses. Instead he sends him out to tell his people all about what God has done for him (verse 39). This nameless individual becomes the first Gentile missionary sent out by Jesus – the first of many (as Luke tells us in Acts).

Questions

1. How do you account for Jesus' serenity through these episodes? Is it possible for us, too, or unique to him?
2. Put yourself in Peter's shoes. What are you feeling through these two stories?
3. What do we learn from these episodes about the world we live in? Imagine that these stories are headline news on the front page. Compose the newspaper editorial, commenting on their significance.

Luke 8:40–56

Lessons in faith

Jesus not only had good news for the poor; he also used them to teach us lessons about trusting him.

After his brief foray into Gentile territory, Jesus returns to a more familiar reaction: a welcoming crowd (verse 40). But it's also a crowd seething with needs, desperation and hope. This section is a 'faith sandwich': Jairus, rich, important and desperate, is the two slices of bread; the woman, unnamed, unnoticed, unclean, is the filling. The simple lesson that we uncover by seeing how the filling affects the bread is the power of faith in Jesus.

Luke draws our attention to just two people in this heaving mass of humanity, and what a contrasting pair they are! Jairus is a ruler of the synagogue, a man of prestige and influence, someone the crowd would part to let through. He comes and falls on his face before Jesus (verse 41) – a formal approach to a noted teacher and holy man. As a Pharisee, Jairus is not sure he approves of Jesus, but he's desperate. His only daughter, twelve years old, is dying (verse 42a). Jesus goes with him at once, pressing his way through the suffocating crowds (verse 42b).

In that mass of people is a woman. While Jairus is pure, she is impure, affected by menorrhagia, an affliction that would have rendered her ritually defiled. So while Jairus is a pillar of the establishment, she is a virtual outcast. Jairus is named; she is anonymous, 'a woman' (verse 43). Jairus comes formally and meets Jesus face to face; she slides anonymously up to his back (verse 44). She's been ill for the twelve years that Jairus' daughter had been alive. She touches the edge of his garment and immediately she is cured (verse 44).

It appears that she wanted to slip away as surreptitiously as she had come – though how she couldn't stop herself from whooping with joy is a mystery! But Jesus stopped dead. In the crush he asked who touched him (verse 45). Everyone denied it – perhaps including the woman, frozen to the spot. Peter tries to point out that it would be a miracle if people weren't touching him. But Jesus knows something has happened; power has been transferred from him to a needy person.

There is a hush in the narrative between verses 46 and 47. Will the woman succumb to fear, or declare her faith? She has much to lose: the crowd holds terrors for her because of her social position, her medical condition that rendered her and those she touched unclean, and the fact that the longer she stayed frozen in her silence, the more jeopardy the little dying girl was in.

She comes forward, falls at Jesus' feet and confesses everything (verse 47). What courage she displays at this point! And what a reward she receives from Jesus! In the hearing of everybody, he declares that her faith has made her well: she can go in peace, knowing the wholeness and well-being of God's kingdom (verse 48).

The joy of the moment is shattered by messengers from Jairus' house, bringing the feared news that his daughter has died (verse 49). Jesus urges him to learn the lesson of the woman. What a thing to ask of a ruler of the synagogue! His daughter is dead, but Jesus wills him to go on believing: 'The situation is as desperate as this woman's was; can you believe like her?'

When they reach the house the funeral has started (verse 52), but Jesus sweeps the mourners out. Taking with him his three closest friends and the parents, he enters the girl's room (verse 51). The mourners laugh in scorn and derision at Jesus' statement that the girl is asleep, not dead; they know a corpse when they see one (verse 53).

Can Jairus keep hold of the lesson he's learned from the nameless woman, or will his fear swamp his faith? The child is raised – Luke's wording confirming that she had indeed died (verse 55) – and the parents are urged not to shout about it from the rooftops (verse 56). They were 'afraid' at what had happened, as the disciples were in the boat (8:25), and the Gerasenes were (8:37); but their fear was a mixture of awe, amazement and faith. Perhaps Jesus tells them to keep quiet because talking about his faith openly might put Jairus in a difficult position with his fellow-Pharisees.

This ruler of Israel had learned a lesson in faith from a woman. Women were virtually invisible in this society. Yet frequently Luke holds them up as models of faith, examples of the poor who responded to Jesus' good news. In 7:36–50 a woman is a model of thankfulness; in 10:38–42 a model of learning; in 18:1–8 a model of prayer; in 21:1–4 a model of giving (cf. 8:1–4); in 23:27–31 women model repentance.

Women are even a picture of God in action: 13:31–35; 15:8–10.

The key point is that the recipients of good news whose lives are changed through their encounter with Jesus become people through whom others encounter him too.

Questions

1. What risks are you prepared to take to bring your need to Jesus?
2. What was Jairus thinking and feeling as Jesus spoke with the woman?
3. How can we ensure that we pay as much attention to anonymous women as we do to important men like Jairus?

Luke 9:1–17

Partners in Jesus' mission

The twelve had been with Jesus for some time. Now it's time for them to participate in his ministry. How will their faith measure up to this new test?

 Luke has hardly focused on the twelve since Jesus called them out of the wider band of disciples (6:12–16; 8:1). Now they take centre stage in a section which is as much about the quality of their faith as it is about going out on mission. The two parts of this section are linked by 'bread': in verse 3 the twelve are told not to take any with them; in verse 13 they are challenged to feed the great multitude with only five loaves. In between comes the

first hint of official (Roman) hostility to Jesus (verses 7–9), which casts a dark pall over the events and invests the feeding of the five thousand men (verse 14a) with a political significance.

Jesus sends the twelve as his emissaries (verses 1–2, cf. 4:36), a foretaste of what's to come in Acts 2. More specifically, they are sharing Jesus' ministry of proclaiming release in word and deed to the poor and oppressed. Luke is keen to stress that, though God's purpose of extending his saving reign to all is being fulfilled in Jesus, others have a role in proclaiming it. This will be the theme of his second book (Acts). It is foreshadowed here (cf. 5:10; 10:1–11).

The command to 'take nothing' will be revoked in 22:35–36 and seems not to apply in Acts. Jesus assumes that in Galilee the twelve will enjoy the same welcome that he has. But it is also a test of their young faith. God will provide all that they need – clothing, shelter, food (verse 3; cf. 11:3; 12:22–34). Do they believe it? They are to accept whatever hospitality is offered. But if they are not welcomed, they are not to pick a fight (verse 5). Jesus has suffered rejection (4:28–30), so the twelve might do too. Making an issue of rejection could draw the unwelcome attention of the powers that be, which at this stage in Jesus' ministry would be a distraction.

Shaking the dust from your feet (verse 5) was a gesture of self-purification often practised by Jews when travelling in Gentile lands. Recommending the disciples do it where they are not welcomed is yet another indication that Jesus is redefining the people of God not along ethnic lines, but solely on the basis of response to him and his messengers.

The twelve travel throughout Galilee, but no further. (Apart from the foray across the lake, Luke has Jesus firmly anchored in Galilee until 9:51, when his decisive journey south begins.) And word reaches Herod. Perhaps the 'all that was going on' (verse 7) refers to the whole of Jesus' ministry, but it is more likely to refer to the mission of the twelve. An isolated teacher-healer is of only passing interest to a king, unless, like John, he offers a direct challenge (3:19–20). But when that teacher sends out others to spread his message, it begins to look like a movement, a threat.

At this stage Herod is merely perplexed (verse 7) and asking questions (verse 9). He's even keen to see Jesus. Later his attitude will harden (13:31–33; 23:7–11; Acts 4:27). Herod's question is the key one that hangs over this part of Luke (from 4:14 onwards). It will be answered by and for the twelve in the next section (9:18ff.). It is asked by all who come into contact with Jesus.

The twelve return and Jesus wants to take them on retreat. They withdraw to the area around Bethsaida, one assumes to pray and recharge their batteries. But that will have to wait until verse 18, because the crowd follows them. And just as the twelve have been welcomed, so Jesus welcomes the crowd, despite the interruption it represents to his plans. The arrival of the crowd also serves to delay the answer to Herod's question (verse 9) again until verses 18–20. And yet the events that unfold because the crowd is there point to an answer to that question which the king will not want to hear.

The miracle of the loaves and fishes is a startling revelation of the identity of Jesus. But it is also a test of the disciples' faith, as verses 12–14 show. The twelve urge Jesus to send the crowd away so they can get something to eat (verse 12). Jesus suggests the twelve feed them (verse 13). But he knows they have nothing, because he sent them off with nothing (verse 3). The twelve ought to have remembered that once, Jesus had provided fish enough for a feast, even when they didn't need it (5:1–11); surely they could expect him to come up with something now. But no. The twelve absurdly suggest they go into town to buy food for this lot (verse 13b) – despite having no money (verse 3).

At this point Jesus takes control of the situation, but includes the twelve in what he does. They organized the crowd's seating arrangements (verse 14) and they distribute the food (verse 16b). They even clear up afterwards (verse 17). Jesus surely intends them to learn not only through what they see and hear but also through what they do under his watchful eye.

Jesus acts as the host at any Jewish meal table would: he

gives thanks, breaks the bread and distributes the food to his guests (verse 16). In doing this the host of a meal was saying that all at his table were welcome as his friends. Jesus is including this great crowd into his wider circle of friends regardless of their status. There is no reference to ritual washing or purification taking place, or to the fish and bread being tithed. The meal is a sign that all and sundry were welcome at Jesus' table; it is an act of inclusion. Of course, to an on-looking king, aware of his nation's history, the meal could also look like the mustering of an army.

For the miraculous feeding in the wilderness ties Jesus firmly to Israel's prophetic tradition, especially Elisha (2 Kings 4:42–44), and to the time of the exodus, Israel's moment of liberation from slavery (Exodus 16:4–36). In John's Gospel the people see clearly what's happening here: they try to make him king at this point (John 6:14–15).

Luke's focus is more narrowly on the disciples. There was one basket of leftovers for each of the twelve (verse 17) – proof that God could provide for those who had faith.

Questions

1. Are the twelve really ready to be sent out on mission? Are we?
2. What is Jesus trying to teach the disciples through the feeding of the five thousand? Are we willing to learn that lesson?
3. Sending out emissaries, feeding an army in the desert ... Put yourself in Herod's shoes: what do you make of Jesus?

Luke 9:18–36

Seeing Jesus as he really is

It's not enough to know who Jesus is. As the disciples discover, they have a lot to learn about Jesus' mission, and theirs.

 This episode, coming at the end of Jesus' Galilean ministry, is a turning-point in Luke's story. The question of who Jesus is, which has hung over all the stories Luke has so far told us, is finally answered for the first time by a human being (18–22; demons have known all along but have been forbidden to tell). Jesus can now shift from merely calling people to follow him, and begin to flesh out what following him entails (verses 23–27). He can also give his closest followers a glimpse of who he really is and why he's come (verses 28–36).

At last Jesus is able to get away with the twelve and possibly others (verse 18, cf. 10). The disciples have clearly heard the same things as Herod's advisors (verse 19, cf. 7–8). But while Herod's camp is confused, the disciples are growing more certain. None more than Peter. He has come a long way in his understanding (see 5:8–9; 8:22–25; 9:12–17). Here he represents the rest of the twelve; they must have talked about this among themselves as they were on the road. And we mustn't overlook the fact that this conversation follows Jesus' prayer and that Peter's answer is based as much on revelation as it is on intuition and observation (cf. Matthew 16:17).

Jesus' command to the disciples not to tell anyone (verse 21) makes perfect sense. We don't know what Peter meant by the word 'Christ'; it was a pretty fluid idea in first-century Israel. But a key component was almost certainly some kind of military king who would lead an army against Rome, free the people and establish the rule of God in the land. Jesus definitely didn't want Peter telling people that's what he'd be doing!

Jesus prefers the title 'Son of Man' to 'Christ' (see p. 191) because he can give it the kind of meaning he wants. His mission, he tells the disciples, involves suffering, betrayal, death and ultimately vindication by God (verse 22). Though popular now with the mass of ordinary people, Jesus was already treated with suspicion by their leaders – the Pharisees, the elders, the chief priests and the teachers of the law (e.g. 6:11). This suspicion is hardening all the time into outright opposition. For the first time Jesus says that this will lead to his death.

As the disciples are digesting this, Jesus spells out the nature of discipleship already hinted at in 6:22–23. Clearly, if Jesus' mission will result in his suffering, those who follow him are also likely to suffer. Jesus describes this as a daily crucifixion (verse 23). To his first hearers, the cross was not so much a symbol as an all too real means of execution. If it symbolized anything, it was the ultimate power of Rome to force its way on the world. Jesus calls his followers to deny themselves, not for Rome's sake, but for his.

We are all faced with choices about how we live, he continues (verses 24–26). If we choose safe lives that accept the world as it is – the world of the chief priests and their Roman overlords, the world of exploitation and oppression – we'll lose our lives. To live this way is to live in opposition to God and his purposes, now being revealed in Jesus. If we follow Jesus, however, and remain faithful to him and his way of life whatever opposition we face, we'll live lives that, though touched with suffering, will ultimately be vindicated by God.

We don't know what the disciples thought about all this, though we get a none too flattering glimpse in the next section. It is a theme that Jesus constantly returns to (9:44; 11:29–32; 12:50; 13:31–35; 17:25; 18:31–33; 20:9–18; 22:19–20, 28; 24:7, 46–47).

Having looked forward to the day of judgment and final

vindication (verse 26), Jesus declares that some of his followers are about to get an insight into what this is all about. Sure enough, a week later (verse 28; Luke is unusually precise), Jesus, Peter, James and John go off together to pray on a mountain.

What we know as the 'transfiguration' is a glimpse of what the future holds for Jesus – both the suffering and the glory – wrapped in God's confirmation to the disciples (including Peter) that Jesus is indeed the Christ, the Son of God.

The appearance of Moses and Elijah (verses 30–31a), the former representing the law, the latter the prophets (that is, the whole of the Old Testament revelation) is highly significant. Moses had spoken of one like him who would come (Deuteronomy 18:15), while Elijah was the prophet most closely associated with the end of the world and the coming of God's kingdom in all its fullness. That these two have come to converse with Jesus indicates that he is indeed the culmination of the Old Testament's witness and the one through whom God will fulfil his promises and purposes.

But their topic of conversation is even more significant. They speak of Jesus' departure, but the word is literally 'exodus' (verse 31b). This fleshes out the words of Jesus to his disciples about his dying in Jerusalem (verse 33c, cf. 22). His death will be the start of a new movement of liberation. As Moses had led the exodus of Israel from slavery in Egypt to freedom in the promised land, so Jesus is going to lead God's new people – those who believe in him and his message – out of slavery to the ways of the world, represented by the priests and Rome, to the freedom of life in God's kingdom.

As ever, Peter nods off during the prayer time (verse 32), but the bright light and voices wake him and he blurts out something about holding an impromptu Feast of Tabernacles, the Jewish festival that looked forward to the coming of God's kingdom. It's a pretty dumb thing to say (verse 33c), since Moses is dead and Elijah had been whisked off to heaven in a chariot – but he probably feels he has to say something.

No sooner has he spoken than the scene goes dark and they are terrified (verse 34). God himself has come to confirm all that Jesus has said with the words that he'd used privately at Jesus' baptism (cf. 3:22), adding that because of this, the disciples should listen to him (verse 35).

Then suddenly, the disciples and Jesus are alone, and everything has returned to normal. The three can't talk about what they've seen (36b) – some experiences are too big and too private. But it ought to have left its mark on them in their understanding of what Jesus was about. The next section suggests that this isn't the case.

Questions

1. What kind of 'freedom' or liberation comes with membership of God's kingdom? See Galatians 5:1. Make a list of the things Jesus frees us from now or later in heaven.
2. Why do you think Peter and his friends fell asleep?
3. How would you reply to someone who said that a weak and rejected figure like Jesus of Nazareth (verse 22) could not possibly be God incarnate?

Prayer

Luke devotes a lot of space to describing both Jesus' own prayer life and his teaching about prayer. Look at what he says and ask yourself: if Jesus, the perfect man, needed to pray, how much more do we?

Jesus' prayer life

3:21	At his baptism.
5:16	Habitually.
6:12	Before appointing the twelve.
9:18	On retreat.
9:28–29	At the transfiguration.

11:1–2   His example prompted the disciples to copy him.
22:41–45 In Gethsemane when he was in need.
23:34   When he was being crucified.

What do we learn from Jesus' practice about praying continually?

Jesus' teaching about prayer

6:28   Pray for enemies.
10:2   Pray for evangelism.
11:1–13   Prayer is effective because God is generous.
18:1–8   Persist in prayer.
18:9–14   Be honest in prayer.
20:47   Don't show off when you pray.
22:40, 46 Pray when you're being tempted.

If you are doing this in a group, survey all these passages (perhaps sharing them round the group) and then put together a 'Ten Commandments of Prayer' to give to new Christians or to pin up on the church wall.

Luke 9:37–50

Lessons in humility

Great spiritual experiences and insights into the nature of God's mission in the world aren't enough. We also need humility of service if we are going to be fruitful for God.

Luke ends his account of Jesus' Galilean ministry on something of a low note: the failure of the disciples in just about every area. They fail in ministry (verses 37–43a). They fail in their understanding of Jesus (verses 43b–45). And they fail in their grasp of discipleship (46–50). In doing this, Luke shows the necessity of Jesus' long and fateful journey to Jerusalem (9:51 – 19:27), giving him the time he needs to mould the twelve into a band of faithful disciples who'll be able to take his mission forward after his return to heaven.

While Peter, James and John have been on the mountain with Jesus, the other nine apostles and the rest of the disciple band have been down with the crowds (verse 37). As soon as the four return, trouble rears its head in the form of a demonized child (verse 38). The description of what the spirit does to this only son is heartbreaking (verse 39). But so is the failure of the disciples to deal with the boy (verse 40, cf. 9:1).

Jesus explodes with exasperation – not at the man or at the crowd, but at his disciples. He likens his followers to the generation who'd been unable to make their mind up about Jesus and John the Baptist (7:31–35). Had the disciples really learned nothing from their time with Jesus, their close observation of his works and words? Clearly not. These are harsh words indeed.

Verse 42 suggests the spirit's hold on the boy is very great, but Jesus dismisses it with a word and gives the healed child back to his father, once again demonstrating that his mission is to bring release to all who are bound (cf. 4:18–19). But the healing is almost an aside to Jesus' stern rebuke of his disciples. The crowd is amazed and overawed, but even as they are marvelling at what Jesus has done, he is warning his disciples to get serious.

'Beware of being sucked in by all the adulation,' is what he's saying in verse 44. The disciples appear to be basking in their status as right-hand men to the chosen king (as verse 46 shows all too clearly). They are behaving as a new in-crowd, a new group of Pharisees, excluding others (verse 49). But for all their talk and bravado, they don't seem to achieve much. They couldn't even perform a simple exorcism.

Jesus reiterates that his mission, and by implication their

discipleship, is about suffering (verse 44). And now Luke tells us clearly what he didn't say in the previous section: the disciples don't get it at all (verse 45). God's Messiah is coming to rule, not to die, they thought; to unite the people behind him, not to divide them and be rejected. The true nature of Jesus' mission is hidden from them by their own preconceptions and unwillingness to have them challenged by what they see and hear. They are in grave danger of living up to Isaiah 6:9-10 despite having been let in on the secrets of the kingdom (8:10). And whereas before they would ask questions (8:9), now they are afraid to do so, perhaps because they don't want to hear the answers.

Far from grasping what Jesus has been saying, they fight among themselves about who is the top dog (verse 46). This won't be the last time it happens (see 22:24-30). So Jesus takes a child – symbol of the poor, marginalized people that he has come to serve; perhaps even the child he's just healed after the disciples' failure to do so – and uses him as an example of what it means to be a disciple.

Three times Jesus uses the word 'welcomes' (verse 48). In the world, people welcome only those of equal status or higher. In the world, greatness is measured by how many people are beneath you, lower down the ladder of achievement and prestige. Jesus knocks the ladder away. He says that if you welcome this child, this representative of those with no status, you welcome him. The disciples knew that Jesus had authority and power; indeed, some had glimpsed his glory and majesty which were currently veiled (verses 28-36). Jesus was standing notions of greatness on their head by identifying himself, and God, with the marginalized (verse 48b). Greatness is about being where God is (verse 48c).

John, who'd been on the mountain of transfiguration, ignores all that Jesus has just said. He speaks up about stopping an 'outsider' from doing the kinds of things the disciples had just proved themselves incapable of doing. Everything Jesus has done and said since the Nazareth sermon (4:14ff.) is being contradicted here. How can the disciples have grasped so little of what he's about?

It is likely that this unnamed exorcist was part of the wider band of disciples. Perhaps he was someone who'd heard Jesus, responded with faith, and spoke about him wherever he went. What John and the other eleven were doing was drawing a line and creating a new 'in-crowd' – just as the Pharisees had done – which created levels of status within the band of disciples. Far from grasping that Jesus' mission is about welcoming any and all who are prepared to put their faith in him, especially those deemed to have no status by the world around them, the disciples were busy creating a whole new alternative status system with themselves at the centre around Jesus.

It will take Jesus and his motley band some time to travel from Galilee in the north to Jerusalem in the south for his showdown with the powers that be. He will use this time to mould his disciples into people who will faithfully serve him by carrying on his mission of reaching out to the poor. Can he succeed?

Questions

1. How can the disciples get it so wrong after they got it so right earlier? Think of times when this has been true of you.
2. Why don't the disciples grasp what Jesus is saying about his impending suffering?
3. How can we translate Jesus' words about greatness into the way our churches are run and our countries are governed?

THE JOURNEY IN:
Jesus heads for
Jerusalem

Luke 9:51 – 19:27

Stop and look

The travel narrative is unique to Luke. He uses it to do two significant things.

The first is to introduce material that no other gospel writer gives us. Many of the encounters – for instance with Mary and Martha and Zacchaeus – are unique to Luke. It is also in the travel narrative that Luke includes such parables as the good Samaritan, the prodigal son, and the rich man and Lazarus, again unique to Luke.

The second major purpose of this section is to flesh out what Jesus means when he calls people to follow him. Discipleship is the key theme of these chapters. So we see Jesus calling people to join him on his journey and spelling out what this will involve. But even more importantly, we see Jesus moulding his existing disciples (who seemed to have lost the plot at the end of the Galilean ministry) into a group of people who could be entrusted with taking his mission on to the ends of the earth after he'd returned to heaven.

The journey Luke narrates is a bit of a meander. And having told the first part of his story at breakneck speed, the pace slows once the journey gets underway (the first section has an urgency lacking in subsequent ones). There are fewer healings and much more concentration on Jesus the teacher as he fills out what life in the kingdom of God is like and how its citizens should live.

The journey to Jerusalem begins with Jesus spelling out for his disciples, would-be disciples and us exactly what following him entails.

There is an urgency about this section. Jesus is constantly on the move in a series of rapid-fire encounters with disciples and would-be disciples. The journey to Jerusalem begins (verse 51) and is reinforced by words that suggest movement: 'heading' (verse 53), 'walking' (verse 57), 'follow' (verses 57–61). There is a foretaste of the rejection that awaits him at his destination (verse 53). And so there is a reiteration of the cost of being a disciple in the context of such rejection (verses 57–62).

Jesus has told his disciples that he is going to Jerusalem and will be rejected by his people, killed by the Romans and raised by God (verses 22, 44). Now with steely determination (that is the force of the word rendered 'resolutely' in verse 51) he strikes out southwards from Galilee to the capital. Luke sets the journey in a cosmic context by telling us that the time for Jesus 'to be taken up to heaven' was approaching. He is seeing the cross, resurrection and ascension almost as a single act. It is Jesus' destiny to confront the powers in the land and the spiritual powers that oppose God's rule, and through that to be vindicated. In Daniel's vision, the Son of Man was taken up to heaven (Daniel 7:13–14; see 'The Son of Man', p. 191).

Everything that happens on the road happens in the context of Jesus' impending vindication. This gives the whole section an urgency and solemnity that we always need to bear in mind.

Jesus is moving out of the territory where he is well known into Samaritan territory (see 'Who were the Samaritans?' on p. 102). The messengers he sends (verse 52) were members of his band of disciples. They were given a frosty reception because Jesus wasn't stopping, just passing through on his way to Jerusalem. Samaritans didn't worship in Jerusalem or look to the Jewish capital for anything. Clearly, Jesus wasn't 'one of them' as far as they were concerned, and so he wasn't welcome.

The incident is a foretaste of the rejection Jesus was about to suffer at the hands of his own people. It was also a reminder to his disciples that not everyone will treat them as returning heroes. Jesus has already been rejected (as well as welcomed) in Galilee (4:28–30). His disciples will be rejected (as well as received) when they take his message to the wider world (as Luke tells us in Acts; e.g. 17:1–9).

James and John think it's time for judgment. After all, they are followers of the king, the Messiah. If people reject him, they should be punished. There is a strong echo of Elijah's ministry in this whole section, as the NIV note to verse 54 reminds us. The background here is 2 Kings 1, where, because King Ahaziah refuses to welcome the word of God through Elijah, he is judged – after several of his messengers sent to confront the prophet are consumed by fire from heaven.

But James and John still haven't grasped what Jesus is about. He rebukes them and moves on (verses 55–56). Now is not a time for judgment; it's a time for salvation. There is an opportunity for any and all who want to respond to Jesus' message and experience the rule of God in their lives. Jesus is on a journey to his destiny, and as he makes his way he gives everyone the opportunity to join him. Their response is between them and God. Jesus' duty, and by implication the disciples' duty, is to preach the message.

Not all rejected Jesus. Jesus was calling people to join his band (verse 59; we assume he was issuing the invitation to everyone). And some were giving a qualified 'yes'. So Jesus spells out the 'all or nothing' nature of discipleship, not just for these would-be disciples, but also for those who've been following him for a while, especially the twelve. Again, Jesus' encounters remind us of when Elijah called Elisha three times to follow him (2 Kings 2:1–6).

To the first man he says that discipleship means giving up everything (verses 57–58). As we saw with Levi (5:27–32), this has more to do with giving over control of what we own to Jesus, rather than merely leaving it to one side. Jesus here says that he has nothing and has to trust God for all his daily needs – food, shelter, clothes. This is a theme that Jesus will return to in more detail (12:22–34).

To the second, Jesus says that allegiance to him is more important than loyalty to family (verses 59–60). The would-be disciple is saying to Jesus that he has to remain at home serving his father until his father dies. Then he will be free to follow. Jesus is saying that the kingdom of God is here now. Now is the time to follow. Those who are not alive to this prospect can stay at home and do funerals. But those who hear the message and believe must act now by going and preaching this message to others (verse 60b), whatever the consequences for family life and arrangements (see 12:51–53).

To the third, Jesus also says that he comes before family (verses 61–62). But the focus here is on authority. The word translated 'say good-bye' (verse 61) means 'take my leave of'. The man is saying that he will follow Jesus if his family give their permission. Jesus' response is simple: just as ploughing is a precise art that requires our full and undivided attention or we'll make a complete shambles of it, so discipleship requires that we focus on Jesus and his authority alone. If we gaze all around us and take our cues from anyone else, even our family, we'll quickly go wrong and lose our way.

We don't know how any of these would-be disciples responded after Jesus laid out the cost of discipleship. Luke leaves it open for us to fill in the answers. Will we follow Jesus, having heard these words?

Questions

1. Jesus doesn't make it easy for the three would-be disciples to follow him. Why not?
2. What are the consequences for our family life of following Jesus?
3. How do we present the call to discipleship in our evangelism? Is it ever right to make following Jesus look attractive, or will this distort the truth?

Who were the Samaritans?

In Jewish eyes the Samaritans were half-breeds, ethnic traitors, bad guys. When the nation was divided [after King Solomon died], Samaria was originally the name for the capital of the Northern Kingdom founded by Omri (1 Kings 16:21–24). Samaritans intermarried with other peoples in the region. They even worshipped at a different site, Mount Gerizim (John 4:20–24). Many recognized only the Pentateuch as inspired. Traditionally Jews and Samaritans were hostile to one another. (Darrell Bock, *Luke*, IVP, 1994)

Luke tells us about Samaritans who rejected Jesus here in 9:53. Elsewhere he alone has the parable of the good Samaritan, where a hated Samaritan turns out to be better at keeping the law of Israel than a priest and a Levite (10:25–37); and he alone tells us of the ten lepers Jesus healed, only one of whom came back to say thank you – and he was a Samaritan (17:11–19).

The kingdom of God is coming through the ministry of Jesus. People need to hear so that they have a chance to respond. Jesus' disciples have the privilege of sharing that work with all its joy and pain.

Despite their slowness to grasp the full meaning of Jesus' message (9:37–50), the disciples are again sent out to proclaim that message in the towns and villages of Israel. There is no hint here that the seventy-two are sent beyond Israel's borders, though Jesus' words about Gentile cities (verses 13–14) paves the way for the mission of the church to the ends of the earth that Luke recounts in Acts.

The task is urgent. The harvest is ready and could rot in the field unless it is gathered in. So Jesus says his followers should both pray for workers and go to be workers themselves, gathering in the harvest (verse 2). But whereas, when the twelve were sent out (9:1ff.), the mood was one of optimism and assurance of welcome, now the probability of rejection is more to the fore (verse 3).

The disciples are given the same instructions about what to take (verse 4, see 9:3). They're also urged not to spend time in small-talk on the road; there just isn't time (verse 4b). Likewise they are told to stay in one place, and if they are not received to move on (see on 9:4–5).

But now Jesus sounds a solemn note of the consequences of rejecting his message (verses 12–16). The sin of Sodom was the sin of not giving hospitality, of not welcoming God's messengers. That had dire consequences for Sodom, and it would have dire consequences for any place rejecting the disciples (see Genesis 19:1–23; Isaiah 3:9; Ezekiel 16:48).

And Jesus gives us an insight into what his real reception had been in the towns of Galilee. For while he had been welcomed, indeed fêted, for his miraculous signs and gracious words, it appears that beneath the superficial openness there had been little repentance in Chorazin, Bethsaida or Capernaum (cf. 8:11–21). He adds that rejecting Jesus or his messengers is the same as rejecting God and his purposes. So what Luke has told us is true of the Pharisees could be true of many of the ordinary people who heard him gladly but failed to repent.

Luke tells us nothing of the mission of the seventy-two. They are sent and they return (verse 17) full of joy and excitement. What a contrast with the picture of the disciples in 9:37–50! Their reference to demons indicates that they were pursuing the same mission of proclaiming release to captives and the coming of the reign of God that Jesus was (4:18–19; 10:8). Sharing their joy, Jesus reminds the disciples of the authority he's given them (verse 19)– something Luke does not tell us at the beginning of this section (but cf. 9:1) – but then also reminds them that power encounters and successful ministry matter less than their initial response of faith to the message of the kingdom (verse 20).

Verse 18 is a key verse in this section. The proclamation of the coming of God's kingdom spells the end of Satan's domination of God's world (see 'The kingdom of God', p. 115). When does Satan fall? It is most likely, given that Luke describes the crucifixion as a triumph for the powers of darkness and reports on Satan's activity all the way through Acts, that this fall will happen in the future. Jesus has had a vision of the coming of the kingdom in all its fullness at the day of judgment: Satan and all who are aligned with him (those who reject Jesus' message now) will fall then.

But the unravelling of Satan's kingdom has begun now in the ministry of Jesus, seen in his authority (shared with his disciples) over all the works and forces of the devil (verse 19), and seen in the healings, release from oppression and repentance of some on hearing Jesus' message.

Having strongly rebuked his disciples (9:41, 44, 50, 55),

Jesus now rejoices over them. At last, it seems, they have got it. It had been hidden from them (9:45), but now it has been revealed to them (verse 21). What the disciples seem to have grasped is that power and authority (the things they fought over in 9:46–50) come to them only in the context of suffering and rejection and for the purpose of announcing the coming reign of God, not for their own personal aggrandisement.

In a wonderful saying of reversal, Jesus tells us that the wise don't get it, while those of no status (the poor, infants, babes-in-arms) do get it – because God reveals it to them. Indeed, he delights to do so; it's why he has sent his Son (verse 21). This revelation happens when the disciples pay close attention to Jesus (verse 22). Again he reiterates that this is not for the powerful; they long to have it, so that they can use it to exploit others. Rather it is for the poor. No wonder Jesus tells his followers that they are fortunate (verse 23a, cf. 6:20–23).

Questions

1. In a world of competing faiths, is it right to go and preach Jesus to everyone? What guidance about our methods can we draw from Jesus' teaching?
2. Do we believe that effectiveness in ministry comes only through suffering, or are there short-cuts?
3. How should we treat people who hear our message but fail to respond in the way we hope?

Luke 10:25–37

Learning to be a neighbour

It is hard enough to put ourselves out for those who are part of our group. It is doubly difficult to reach out and help those who aren't like us. But that is what Jesus expects of his followers.

The travel narrative gives Luke the space to include much of the material that is unique to his story, of which this famous parable is a prime example. It is  related to what has gone before, however. Jesus has been talking about discipleship and life in the kingdom. Here he spells out the quality of service that is expected of his followers.

The teacher of the law – quite possibly a priest not on active service (see 'Sects and parties', p. 135) – either interrupts Jesus' conversation with his disciples (verses 23–24) or comes up to the group as they are travelling along the road. His question was a test (verse 25), but Jesus welcomes it because the answer to it is important for everyone listening, especially his disciples.

Jesus' counter-question touched on a very live issue in first-century Judaism, one that he himself would be asked later (see Mark 12:28–34). The lawyer answers it correctly – a subtle reminder of Jesus' authority to interpret the law (verse 28). But when told to go and do it, he asks, 'Who is my neighbour?' (verse 29). This question probes the heart of what Jesus is all about (6:27–36). The lawyer wants to draw boundary lines. Will Jesus let him?

Characteristically, Jesus answers with a parable, a teasing story that draws his questioner in and forces him to confront the issues and answer his own question. It concerns a man on a journey (as Jesus is) who becomes the victim of violence (as Jesus will once he arrives in Jerusalem). Stripped, beaten and left for dead, he lies at the side of the road (verse 30).

A priest (a man just like the lawyer) comes across the unconscious traveller (verse 31). Because the injured man is naked, the priest cannot tell if he is someone who should be helped, if he is 'one of us'. He might already be dead, in which case, if the priest touches him, he'll become ritually unclean. So he moves on. No doubt the lawyer nodded his approval of his colleague's action at this point.

Along comes a Levite, a lesser temple official (verse 32). Knowing the priest is ahead of him, he takes his cue from his superior and doesn't stop. Then a Samaritan – definitely not 'one of us', the lawyer would be thinking – stops, tends the man's wounds, puts him on his own donkey, takes him to an inn, pays for his lodging and ensures he has all he needs to make a full recovery (verses 33–35). Luke's readers will be alert to the fact that the Samaritan 'has pity' (verse 33b) on the wounded traveller, just as Jesus had had pity on the widow of Nain (7:13). But what was the lawyer thinking? This unclean Samaritan has fulfilled the law of love, while the priest and Levite have not.

At the end of his story, Jesus subtly changes the issue. The lawyer had asked, 'Who is my neighbour?' (verse 29). Jesus now asks which one had been a 'neighbour' to the man. In keeping with his teaching that we should love our enemies and do good to those who persecute us (6:27–36), Jesus tells us that the mugged Jew found that it was his enemy, not his fellow-countrymen, who proved to be his neighbour. Furthermore, he says that this outsider, this enemy, is a model for this good Jewish lawyer to follow (verse 37b).

The point, says Jesus, is not that we help only those who are in our group. Rather, it is that we help anybody and everybody who needs it, because that is what Jesus is doing through his ministry. Indeed, that is God's intention in sending Jesus (1:54–55, 76–79; 15:20) .

And again Luke leaves the end of the story hanging. We

know clearly what the lawyer should do in response to his own question. But we don't know whether he did it. This is Luke's way of ensuring we ask ourselves the same question Jesus asked of the lawyer (verse 36).

Questions

1. The hostility between Jews and Samaritans was very sharp. Can you think of modern equivalents which would bring the point of the parable home vividly in your culture or society?
2. What does this parable teach about the willingness to receive love and care, as well as to give it? Why is this sometimes so hard?
3. Think about the four aspects of ourselves with which we must love God in verse 27. Can you illustrate each of these with an example?

Faith and works

Are we Christians because we *believe* certain things, or because we *do* certain things? Jesus seems to say to the lawyer in this story that what we do matters just as much as what we believe. So just what is the relationship between faith and works?

Look at the following encounters in Luke's story. What does each of them tell us about

▶ faith (what we believe, who we trust)?

▶ works (how we live our lives)?

▶ the relationship between them?

Make notes under each heading and compare them at the end.

From your reading of Luke, what would you say were the main differences between what Jesus said about faith and works and what the Pharisees said? Whose view is more common in the church?

Luke 10:38 – 11:13

Lessons in spirituality

The demands of discipleship are being spelled out by Jesus as he travels. But here we glimpse the resources available to make a life of discipleship possible: learning and praying are the marks of true spirituality.

The theme of hospitality links the story of Jesus in the home of Mary and Martha to what has gone before (verses 13–16). But hospitality is not just about welcome, it is also about listening and responding to Jesus' message. Hence the contrast between Mary and Martha.

Martha welcomes Jesus to her home (verse 38) but finds the responsibilities of hosting – laying on a meal for a party of at least thirteen, possibly more – means that she can't pay her guest much attention, and tells him so (verse 40). Her sister, however, doing nothing to help Martha, sits at Jesus' feet (verse 39). The scene is set for a significant word from Jesus on who is right. Luke doesn't disappoint us. Notice that three times Jesus is called 'Lord' and that Mary's posture – at his feet – emphasizes his authority as teacher.

Gently he rebukes Martha. Hospitality is not about good meal preparation, but listening to Jesus (8:11–21; 10:8–16). The shock of the story is that Mary, a woman, is welcome at the feet of the teacher – indeed, encouraged to be there, to the neglect of her domestic duties. Women were generally not taught much about the law. In that respect they were 'the poor' who need to be 'released' from the 'oppression' of ignorance and welcomed as equals into the band of disciples (4:18–19; 8:2–3).

Martha is distracted from what really matters (verse 40). She has not grasped the urgency of the time (verses 2–4) and so is caught up in things that matter less than listening to Jesus. Mary, by contrast, has chosen 'what is better' (verse 42). Discipleship is possible only if we sit at the feet of Jesus.

The theme of learning from Jesus links this scene with the one that follows it. Luke has told us several times about Jesus' prayer life (see 'Prayer', p. 92). Now his praying is a spur to his disciples to ask him to teach them to pray. It was common for a teacher to pass on his methods to his disciples (verse 1b). Clearly, the disciples had made the connection between Jesus' power and the time he spent praying.

What he taught his disciples has come to be known as 'the Lord's Prayer'. It is less an actual prayer to recite (though that is no bad thing) than a model of how we should pray. It is similar to the Qaddish, an Aramaic prayer used at every synagogue service in Jesus' day.

It is Jesus who reveals God to his disciples as Father (10:22) – hence the start of his model prayer (verse 2b). He will illustrate what the fatherhood of God is like in a moment (verses 5–13). But first he urges his disciples to see the focus of their praying as the coming of the rule of the gracious Father (verse 2c), within which all our needs will be met (verse 3) and our sins forgiven (verse 4a). And if we are forgiven, we will forgive – though we need help to do that (verse 4b). The disciples are learning that life on the road with Jesus can be difficult, so they need strength to stand firm. They need to pray that testing times won't come (verse 4c).

The trouble with lessons in prayer is that people often think that all they need is the right technique and that will get them the answers they're looking for. Jesus is not teaching a 'how to' of prayer, but rather a 'who to'. So he follows up this model prayer with more insight into the character of the one the disciples are praying to: his Father.

The parable of the friend at midnight (verses 5–8) is a parable of contrast. Jesus is not saying that God will give us what we want only if we badger him and rob him of sleep. Rather, like the parable of the persistent widow (18:1–8), Jesus is saying that God will willingly give us all that we need, whatever time of the day or night we come with our request. Hence his appeal to his followers to ask, seek and knock (verses 9–10). The verbs in verse 9 are in the present tense, which indicates that this asking, seeking and knocking is a continuous activity that we do in the certainty that God will answer (verse 10).

Then Jesus contrasts his Father with human fathers. Fishes and snakes could look similar, as could an egg and a curled-up scorpion (verses 10–11). But that isn't the point. The point is that it is absurd to think that even evil people like us will intentionally harm our children (verse 13a). Arguing from the lesser to the greater, Jesus says that God will give us everything we need to live the life of discipleship he has called us to.

It was expected that the Holy Spirit would be poured out as a sign that the kingdom had arrived. It was something God did, not that we asked for. Here Jesus fleshes out what praying 'Your kingdom come' means: that God will come to us with all the resources of his Spirit. This is evidence that the new age, so long awaited, had at last dawned. It is also the first mention of a theme that will become increasingly important through the rest of Luke's story (see especially Acts 1:8; 2:1–4).

Questions

---

1. What role do women have in learning and teaching in your church? Is anyone excluded from hearing the good news?
2. Look at how Jesus prays, and how he teaches his disciples to pray. Can we teach one another about prayer?
3. What does the passage teach us about our priorities, as a church and as individuals?

Luke 11:14–36

Spiritual warfare

Jesus' ministry divides not just the scribes and the Pharisees but the crowds as well. He is involved in a battle for allegiance. Which way will we jump?

The seemingly abrupt break between this section and what has gone before shouldn't prevent us from seeing that a key theme in both sections is reaction to  Jesus: will he be welcomed or shunned? This section and the next give us a glimpse of the mounting opposition to Jesus, not just among the Pharisees (see 11:37–54), but even among the crowds.

The scene starts familiarly enough: an exorcism results in people being amazed (verse 14). Immediately, however, sceptics emerge from the crowd (verses 15–16). Jesus had hinted that the crowds had not been universally for him in the parable of the sower (8:4–15) and in his words about Galilean towns (10:12–16). But this is the first time Luke records such opposition.

Luke tells us the crowd responded in three ways: amazement (verse 14c), accusation that Jesus was in league with the devil (verse 15) and demands for a sign (verse 16). Jesus deals with each one. But notice that 'amazement', the positive reaction, is dealt with in the middle of the passage (verses 27–28), which enables Luke to put at the heart of the section Jesus' saying that hearing and doing the word of God are what matters.

The second response, that he is driving out demons by the power of the prince of demons (Beelzebub), is given the fullest treatment (verses 17–26). It is plainly absurd for two reasons. One is that a divided kingdom cannot stand (verses 17–18). The other is: if that's how Jesus does it, what about other Jewish exorcists (19)?

But having dismissed the objection, Jesus urges his detractors to believe the evidence of their eyes. Demons are being expelled; doesn't this mean that a greater kingdom is at work? Can that greater kingdom be anything but God's kingdom (verse 20)? This is an issue he returns to in verses 33–36.

He reinforces this interpretation of his actions with an image from contemporary society. People with lots of possessions regularly posted armed guards to prevent their houses being plundered (verses 21–22). The implication of this mini-parable is that Jesus is the strong man who has ransacked Satan's poorly guarded property.

Then he issues the challenge: are you for me or against me (23–26)? First he issues it directly (verse 23), then indirectly through a reference to popular views about the behaviour of demons (24–26). Jesus' interest here is not whether this is an accurate portrait of the life cycle of a demon but whether those exorcised have aligned themselves with the kingdom of God. If not, their prospects are poor (26).

At this point Jesus is interrupted, a device Luke often uses to emphasize the importance of the point about to be made (e.g. 12:13; 13:1). The woman in the crowd suggests that Jesus is a prophet by ascribing great status to his mother (verse 27). But his response is that 'great status'

113

belongs to all those who hear God's word and obey it (verse 28). In context, of course, this refers to those who believe what Jesus has just said about his exorcisms proving that God's kingdom is coming into the world through his ministry – a bold claim, but not as bold as the one he's about to make.

The crowd is swelling (verse 29a) but Jesus has no illusions about it being on his side. Indeed, he uses words already heard in 7:31 and 9:41 in the context of stubborn misunderstanding of his message (verse 29b). Again, in context, there is an irony about telling the crowd that there'll be no sign – for what are his exorcisms and healings, if not signs that he is God's messenger bringing God's rule? But they are blind to it.

So Jesus says the only real sign this crowd will get is the sign of Jonah (verses 29c–30). Clearly, this is a reference forward to Jesus' resurrection after his final rejection by the crowds and their leaders has resulted in his death. It is also probably an allusion to the fact that Jonah preached repentance ahead of judgment, just as Jesus is doing.

He goes on to stress just how fortunate the crowd is to hear him – surely an ironic play on the woman's cry of 'Blessed' (27), again drawing our attention to the key verse 28. Jesus claims to be greater than both Solomon, the father of Israelite wisdom, and Jonah, the prophet whose ministry caused a pagan superpower to repent (verses 31–32).

And this leads him into a direct appeal to his hearers to believe what they are seeing (verses 33–36). In language reminiscent of 8:16–18, which was about hearing, he tells the people actually to look at what's going on. Jesus is the light shining through what he says and does (verse 33). Those who see him respond negatively or positively according to the light they already have. If they are predisposed to write Jesus off as a fraud, then what they 'see' will confirm that (verse 34 – on the basis that in the ancient world the eyes didn't let light in from the outside, but let it out from the inside).

It is our attitude of heart that Jesus is addressing here. Are we open to God acting in this new way through his servant? (verses 35–36)? Again the ball is in our court: the fortunate are the ones who see and hear the word of God and respond positively.

Questions

---

1. How can we guard ourselves and deliver others from the kind of demonic oppression Jesus deals with here?
2. Jesus was not distracted from his task by either praise or opposition. How do we cope with both these? And how do we ensure that we stay focused on the task in hand?
3. Often Christians write off a new move of God as something else. How can we develop healthy eyes (verse 34) to perceive clearly what God is doing in our world?

The kingdom of God

Luke persistently tells us that Jesus preached the 'kingdom of God'. What does this mean?

In the Old Testament God is portrayed as king now, but a king whose reign is not fully acknowledged either in the world or even in Israel. So there is a tension between the kingdom of God being here (the 'now') and the kingdom still being something that will come in the future (the 'not yet'). God is king now over creation (Psalm 29:10) and over Israel (Exodus 15:18; Isaiah 43:15). But one day he will be king over the earth (Zechariah 14:9 and over Israel (Zephaniah 3:14–20) in a fuller sense.

Because of this tension between the 'now' and the 'not yet', there were lots of differing views about what the kingdom was and when it would come in Jesus' day (see 'Sects and parties', p. 135).

► The **conservatives** (Sadduccees, priests and scribes)

said the kingdom comes when we submit to the law of Moses.

▶ The **Pharisees** thought that God would bring his kingdom in his own good time (e.g. Luke 17:20). This was the view shared by most ordinary first-century Jews (cf. Acts 1:6).

▶ The **Essenes** believed that when the time was ripe they would fight as the sons of light to defeat the sons of darkness, especially the Kittim (a code name of the Romans), and hence usher in the kingdom.

▶ The **Zealots** weren't prepared to wait for God. They believed an armed rebellion against the Romans would force God to act to rescue his people and bring in his kingdom. There were lots of minor risings through the first century, leading up to the revolt of AD 66, which was ruthlessly crushed by Rome.

Jesus stepped into this smorgasbord of ideas and expectations with his message of the kingdom (4:43).

▶ **Reign, not realm.** The kingdom is not a geographical place but a statement about who's in charge. It comes near to people (10:9); it's in our midst (17:21); it's about doing God's will (11:2).

▶ **Revealed in Jesus.** In Jesus' ministry the kingdom, the reign of God, is being shown to people (4:16–21; 7:18–23; 11:20; 16:16; 17:20–21). But there is a tantalizing quality to this revelation. The kingdom has not come in its fullness. One day it will (13:22–30; 14:15–24; 22:15–18).

▶ **Radically new.** Someone described God's reign as 'the upside-down kingdom'. We see this quality in the beatitudes (6:20–26), in Jesus' talk about status (9:46–48), in his message that the religious will miss out while the misfits go right on in (14:15–24), in his parables of reversal (15:1–10; 18:9–14), in his welcome to tax gatherers (5:27–32; 19:1–10) and in his message of good news to the poor (4:18–19).

▶ **Requires a response from us.** The kingdom brings division (12:49–53); we cannot sit on the fence (11:23). We enter the kingdom by faith (7:1–10; 9:18–20; 19:1–10). We reject it by rejecting Jesus and his message (6:11; 11:15; 18:18–29).

Luke 11:37–53

Hard words for the religious

The people who found it hardest to hear what Jesus was saying were the religious of his day. Are we similarly in danger of allowing our religious practice to drown out God's voice?

This scene is carefully structured with Jesus entering the house (verse 37) and leaving it (verse 53) and in between engaging in a somewhat one-sided dialogue with his opponents. Three 'woes' to the Pharisees (verses 42, 43, 44) are balanced with three woes to their allies, the scribes or teachers of the law (verses 46, 47, 52).

When Jesus has finished speaking to the crowds, a Pharisee invites him for a meal (verse 37). This indicates that though Jesus and the religious elite were wary of each other, the channels of communication between them were still open. Indeed, as we shall see, Jesus is keen for these people to repent.

His host was surprised that Jesus didn't wash his hands (verse 38). This wasn't about hygiene. Ritual washing was very important for the Pharisees. To do it marked you as an 'insider'. Not doing it marked Jesus as an 'outsider'. Immediately Jesus is divided from the other guests over what made people pure. His comments (verses 39–40) expose the Pharisees, who think they are pure through their rituals, as those who are in fact full of darkness (verses 33–36).

For Jesus, purity – living the kind of life God wanted you to – was about breaking barriers down, not building them up. So instead of fussing over whether dishes had been properly washed, his fellow-diners should have been sharing the food in them with the poor. For Luke, the giving of alms was not just charity; it was an act of social solidarity with those in need: treating them as if they were your family (cf. Acts 2:44–45; 4:32, 34–37) .

Jesus launches into three woes: lampooning the Pharisees' nit-picking tithing of absolutely everything while neglecting to share with the poor out of the abundance they had left (verse 42); ridiculing their love of being seen by an adoring public (verse 43); and suggesting that far from being squeaky clean, they are in fact as 'ritually impure' as a corpse (verse 44). This is not likely to gain Jesus many friends around the table.

And yet he leaves the door open to the repentance of his hearers. If the Pharisees choose to, they can live by the values of the kingdom (verse 41). Furthermore, his words in verse 42 pick up the question he'd been asked earlier about neighbours by the teacher of the law (10:25–37). Jesus is urging his hearers to remember what he'd said then, and to do it (cf. 11:28).

A teacher of the law leaps to the defence of his colleagues, something he might have regretted in view of Jesus' response. The scribe respectfully addresses Jesus as 'Teacher', and points out that Jesus has been anything but respectful (verse 45).

But Jesus continues in the same vein, turning his fire on the scribes. First, he describes them as purveyors of guilt. In their teaching, he says, they add conditions to the law that ordinary people couldn't possibly meet (verse 46). Perhaps he has in mind the ritual washing and purifications surrounding mealtimes, the onerous expectations about tithing or the increasingly ludicrous Sabbath regulations. Their teaching has the effect of excluding people, not including them, he says.

He goes further, however, accusing these keepers of the law of actually rejecting the very message of the law they claim is so precious. They have endorsed their ancestors' persecution of the prophets (see Nehemiah 9:26; Jeremiah 3:20) by metaphorically building tombs for them – i.e. venerating their memory while ignoring their message (verses 47–51). Jesus is not quoting any Old Testament text in verse 49. Rather, he is claiming a greater insight into God's mind than these experts of the law have.

He warns them that they will be held responsible for the rejection of God's prophets down the centuries (verses 50–51) because they too have killed the prophets off, by ignoring their message. Jesus probably has in mind the prophets' prediction of his own coming. For the scribes have rejected him, just as they had rejected John the Baptist (7:29–30) – and worse still, they are stopping others from accepting him (verse 52).

Not surprisingly, perhaps, the reaction of the scribes and the Pharisees is wholly negative. Far from leading to repentance, Jesus' words cement their opposition to him and all he stands for (verses 53–54). His words were more than just a challenge to their lifestyle; they were an assault on their identity, an identity built on a false idea of what God wanted them to be. Seeking to be wise and faithful followers of God, their misunderstanding of the heart of God's message to Israel from Abraham onwards led them to reject the very person who embodied that message to them: Jesus. Is there any danger we'll do the same?

Questions

1. Have we added any rituals or rules to the simple gospel that act as stumbling-blocks to outsiders? How can we get rid of them?

2. Is it ever right for us to speak to people as Jesus speaks to the Pharisees and scribes here? Since their reaction was so negative, did Jesus act wisely?
3. Is religion intrinsically harmful? Is Jesus offering a real alternative?

Luke 12:1–21

Sorting out our allegiance

Following Jesus means standing out from the crowd and not putting our trust in people's opinions or our material possessions. Jesus urges us to see events in this life in the light of God's judgment.

This section and the two that follow it centre on the nature of discipleship in the face of mounting division over Jesus, and in the certainty of God's coming judgment. In it Jesus contrasts the yeast of the Pharisees (12:1) with the yeast of the kingdom (13:20–21), and spells out for his disciples and the crowds what following him will entail.

Jesus emerges from the Pharisee's house into the largest crowd assembled in Luke's story (verse 1) – a fact that emphasizes the importance of this whole discourse. In view of the Pharisees' opposition and the ambivalence of the crowd, Jesus' focus is on his disciples (verse 1c).

Having already catalogued the hypocrisy of the Pharisees (11:38–52), he warns his disciples to guard against it invading them like yeast in a batch of dough. He says that the 'purity' of the Pharisees is driven more by a fear of men and their opinions than by the fear of God (verses 4–5). And that is bound to be exposed (verses 2–3). So, says Jesus, be sure that what you believe is true and not just a matter of popular opinion.

The disciples will inevitably face persecution if they do not follow the Pharisees' example (verse 4, cf. 6:22–23). This is a justifiable cause of anxiety, something Jesus deals with from verse 22. But Jesus stresses that such opposition – human judgment of their allegiance – must be seen in the context of God's judgment (verse 5; a theme that dominates the passage down to verse 21 and resurfaces in verses 35–48). The Pharisees and anyone else who persecutes them (here Luke paves the way for the story of the church in Acts) can hurt only the body. They cannot harm the soul; only God can do that (verse 5).

But God is on the side of the disciples (verses 6–7, cf. 22–34, especially 32). Those who respond to Jesus' message by putting their faith in him and remaining loyal to him, even through tough times, will be cared for by God (verse 7b). Indeed, when they are called to defend themselves, God himself will give them the words they need (verses 11–12).

Those who fail to respond to Jesus' message, however, or those who fall away because of the pressures of discipleship (cf. 8:13), face being disowned by Jesus on the day of judgment (verses 8–9). Clearly, this word is directed mainly at the Pharisees, and hence to encourage the disciples; but it is also a warning to his followers to remain faithful despite the cost. Even more clearly, the Pharisees and their followers among the crowd are the target of verse 10: it's one thing not to believe a messenger (10a), but it's quite another to attribute the work of God to the devil (10b; 11:15, 52).

Then a man interrupts with what appears to be a complete red herring (verse 13). His question displays anxiety about his future. Jesus has been speaking about the natural fear that arises in the context of persecution. But that is just one example of a more general anxiety that can arise when we seek to live by the values of the kingdom. What about our material needs? Jesus contrasts kingdom values with the greed that makes people live for money and material possessions (verse 15). Again he has half an eye on the Pharisees (11:41; 16:14).

Jesus' initial response to the man is highly ironic (verse 14). He is indeed both judge (verse 8) and divider (verses 51–53), though not in the way his questioner thought. Maybe he was a disciple – or someone pondering his response to Jesus, and was already experiencing the effects of the division that Jesus causes in the fact that his brother would not share the family wealth with him. How was he going to live?

Before dealing with the general issue of anxiety, however, Jesus tells a parable that warns about the eternal consequences of greed. Two things stand out in particular in the parable. The first is that Jesus does not condemn the farmer's activity, only his attitude to wealth. It's OK to work hard and prosper. It's not OK to hoard all your wealth for yourself (cf. 11:41). The second is the total selfishness of the farmer: there are eight first-person verbs in the parable and four uses of 'my'. This man feels the whole world revolves around him and his needs. But in the midst of his wealth, he is called to judgment by God and is found to be totally poverty-stricken (verse 21)

The message is simple: greed should not mark the lifestyle of a disciple. Indeed, possessions, far from being a sign of God's blessing (cf. 18:26), are more likely to prevent the disciple from seeking the kingdom. Of course, such a message immediately raises the issue of how the disciple will make ends meet. That is what Jesus turns to in the next section.

Questions

1. Does following Jesus automatically lead to persecution? If we're living unmolested lives, are we doing something wrong?
2. The rich man in the parable was doing the first-century equivalent of providing a pension for himself to secure a comfortable life into old age. What would Jesus say to us about providing for our future through life savings, life assurance or pension plans, if these are open to us?

3. In what way does the Pharisees' response to Jesus help us to understand what blasphemy against the Holy Spirit is? (See also 11:14–36.) How can we ensure we don't do it?

Luke 12:22–48

Handling anxiety in uncertain times

Persecution is only one of the potential snares that can catch a disciple. Being caught up in the affairs of the world is also an acute danger. God gives us the kingdom; what will we do with it?

 Jesus now broadens the focus of his teaching from fear in the teeth of persecution to more general anxiety about making ends meet (verses 22–34), before returning to the theme of living this life in the light of God's coming judgment (verses 35–48).

The interruption from the crowd has enabled Jesus to talk about the peril of greed. If verses 2–12 illustrate the risk of turning out like the rocky soil (8:6, 13), verses 22–34 illustrate the danger of turning out like the weedy soil (8:7, 14). These verses explain for his disciples the meaning of the parable of the rich fool.

He stresses that they shouldn't fret and worry about how they'll have enough to eat and wear (verse 22), for four reasons. First, life is about more than what we have (verse 23). Secondly, nature teaches us, if we'll only look carefully, that God feeds the birds (verse 24) and clothes the flowers of the field (verses 27–28). We are so much more valuable than either (verses 24b, 28b). Thirdly, worry achieves nothing (verses 25–26). It didn't for the farmer in the parable, and it won't for us. Coming sandwiched between the two observations from nature, this saying is the key point of these verses.

Fourthly, our attention should not be trained on these things. Rather, we should be focused on the kingdom (verses 29–31). Worry is rooted in a fundamental misunderstanding of the character of God (11:1–13), such as the pagans have (verse 30a). The disciples ought to know that God generously provides for those who put their trust in him (9:10–17).

So rather than hoard like the rich fool (verses 18–19) or the Pharisees (11:41), the little flock of disciples can live generously, sharing what they have with those in need (Acts 2:44–45; 4:32–37). The treasure that comes our way as we live like this is the depth of our relationships with God and one another, as well as our future salvation.

Seeking God's kingdom rather than our own material well-being means that we'll be alert to what God is doing (verses 35–48). These verses have the twin foci of Jesus' first and second comings – a fact we need to keep in mind if we're going to understand them aright. Verse 35 contains an echo of the Passover (eating with loins girded and no trace of yeast in the house) and hence recalls Jesus' warning to his followers to avoid the Pharisees' yeast (verse 1b).

Jesus contrasts the alertness of his disciples with the inattention of the Pharisees (verses 36–38). The master (Jesus) came and found the disciples ready, so he served them, meeting their needs (verses 22–31; cf. 22:24–30, especially 27). This is indeed good news to the poor, the ministry Jesus has been engaged in since he laid out his manifesto at Nazareth (4:18–19). But the scene of the banquet also has an eye on the future, on the great banquet that the Messiah will throw for all his faithful people when the kingdom of God comes in its fullness. That will be a time when social status, so precious to the Pharisees, will be meaningless. By implication, it should be meaningless now among God's people (9:46–48; 12:32–34).

Still on the theme of being ready, Jesus shifts the focus from the coming of the master to the coming of a thief (verses 39–40) – though *he* is still the subject of these parables. Jesus' coming is unexpected. Again, both the present and the future are in view. His first coming has taken the Pharisees and the crowds (cf. verses 54–59) by surprise. Will his second coming similarly catch his followers off guard?

At this point Peter seeks clarification: who is Jesus speaking to (verse 41)? It's a good question. After all, Jesus has been speaking to his disciples (verses 1, 4, 22), to the crowd (verses 1, 13) and possibly to the Pharisees (verses 1, 15–21). And Jesus answers Peter's question with a question (verse 42). The issue is: will any of his hearers faithfully live up to God's calling to seek his kingdom? (verses 43–44; note that verse 44 anticipates the parable in 19:11–27)? Or will we assume that God's not looking and live for ourselves (verses 45–46)? The self-talk in verse 45–46 reminds us of the rich fool planning his life without reference to God, his kingdom or God's calling on our lives. Such people face terrible punishment (verses 46–48a).

The section ends on a downbeat note: a lot will be expected of those who have been given much. In context this refers to the Pharisees, entrusted with the law and promises of God, who appear to have squandered what they were given. But it also refers to the disciples who've been given the kingdom (verse 32) and all God's gracious provision (verses 22–31). Will we similarly squander it?

Questions

1. The basic error Jesus attacks in this section is not being ready. How can we ensure that we are ready when Jesus meets us in worship? And when he returns as judge?
2. What sort of behaviour is Jesus attacking in verses 45–46 (remembering that this is a 'parable' – we are meant to apply it to other areas of life)? What's the basic error that could make him treat us as unfaithful?
3. Is God a severe judge, or a forgiving father? How can he be both? Is it possible?

Money

Jesus spoke about money more than about any other subject except judgment. And what he said is unsettling, uncomfortable and surprising. It is also largely ignored by Christians in many parts of the world today.

What do you make of the following? If working alone, jot down your thoughts as you go along, then think about the questions at the foot of the section. If working as a group, discuss your findings. You can make use of the material you gather to mount a display at church, or to lead a service, or to review your giving together.

6:24–26	Woe to the rich.
11:39–43	Money corrupts faith.
12:13–21	Faith in money is misplaced.
12:22–34	Money hinders our focus on God, so get rid of it.
14:15–24	Money can't buy you a place at the table – quite the opposite.
16:1–9	Money is an evil power that will control you if you don't control it.
16:19–31	How you use your cash in this life affects your eternal destiny.
18:18–30	Money can stop you entering the kingdom.
19:1–10	What you do with money shows you have entered the kingdom.

▶ Why does Jesus talk about money so much?

▶ What does Jesus' preoccupation with money tell you about the place of your money in your life of discipleship?

▶ Look at what you have – your earnings and possessions. Do they help or hinder your walk with

God? How can you amend the situation for the better? What would Jesus say to us about the relationship between wealthy and poor churches?

Luke 12:49 – 13:21

Corrupting the world for good

Avoiding contamination by the yeast of the Pharisees is only part of our calling. Jesus also wants us to invade the world with the counter-yeast of the kingdom, seen in faithfulness to God and good works.

The note of impending crisis that has been simmering throughout this whole episode now explodes, as Jesus urges the crowd to heed what's happening and repent (verses 49–59). Even when he is asked to comment on a recent political outrage, Jesus doesn't change tack: calamities happen; get right with God before one happens to you (13:1–9). The final scene gives the positive reason for repentance: Jesus has come to bring the kingdom of release for the poor (verses 10–21).

Still speaking to his disciples, Jesus reveals the anguish of his heart (verses 49–50). He has come to bring judgment, as John the Baptist predicted (3:16–17), but that judgment will fall on him before it falls on anyone else. When Jesus speaks about his impending baptism, he means the cross (verse 50). Jesus knows his death is in the purpose of God (9:30–31); it's the reason for his journey to Jerusalem. But he also knows it will result from the people ultimately rejecting him and will lead to their judgment. And so he talks about conflict arising in families because of him (verses 51–53).

Undoubtedly this caused murmuring among the crowd,

because he turns to speak directly to them (verse 54). They have got to see what's happening before it's too late, he says (verses 55–56). But they can't, because they're infected with the yeast of the Pharisees (hypocrites, verse 56a, cf. verse 1). Judgment is coming; they are in the dock. But the verdict has not been handed down; they could still settle the case before the judge hands out sentence (verses 57–59). That is, they should repent and believe Jesus.

A group in the crowd invites him to comment on a recent Roman atrocity. Perhaps they want to insist that some (the Romans) are more deserving of punishment than others (13:1). But Jesus keeps the focus on the victims of the atrocity (verse 2), and warns his hearers not to draw up lists of heroes and villains (verse 4): all face the judgment of God, so all need to repent (verses 3, 5).

The parable about the fig-tree (verses 6–9) is a reminder to the people (drawn from a rich pool of Old Testament pictures of Israel; e.g. Psalm 80:8–18; Isaiah 5:1–7) – that God is merciful and gives time for people to repent. But his mercy will not last not last for ever: eventually the time will come when putting off a decision will become a decision against.

Luke now tells us that this discourse is happening on a Sabbath (which charges it with even more significance) and in or around a synagogue (verse 10). We don't know when Jesus arrived at the synagogue. But Luke's reason for telling us now is to heighten the tension, as the episode which began in 12:1 rushes to its climax.

In the synagogue is a woman who has been bent double for eighteen years (verse 11). Jesus calls her over and sets her free (verse 12). Here is good news to the poor (a woman), the bringing of 'release' (cf. 4:18–19), and the plundering of Satan's kingdom (verse 16, cf. 11:14ff.). This is the yeast of the kingdom unleashed in the heartland of the yeast of the Pharisees, the synagogue (which might explain why Luke has left it until now to tell us where Jesus is teaching).

Needless to say, the synagogue ruler, a Pharisee, explodes with indignation. There is no need to heal on the Sabbath; Jesus could have healed on any other day of the week. After all, her case was hardly an emergency (verse 14). Such a reaction is an example of the yeast Jesus has warned about (verse 15a, cf. 12:1, 56). The Pharisees, for all their nit-picking Sabbath observance, have not lifted a finger to help this woman in eighteen years – despite leading their animals to water on every Sabbath over that time (verse 15b).

This woman is just as much a part of God's people as the Pharisees (she is a 'daughter of Abraham', verse 16a) just as Zacchaeus is 'a son of Abraham' despite being a tax collector (19:9). Doesn't she deserve to be 'untied' on the Sabbath like a thirsty animal? (Pointedly, Jesus uses the same Greek verb 'untie' in verses 15 and 16.) For isn't the Sabbath a reminder of being set free from slavery in Egypt (Deuteronomy 5:15)? Instead, the Pharisees seem to have turned the Sabbath into a symbol of the bondage they keep people in (cf. 11:46, 52).

The crowd, having been ambivalent about Jesus, is momentarily united in praise at what he's done (verse 17). But Jesus wants his disciples to mark the lesson of this healing. The kingdom of God, manifest now in a solitary Galilean preacher and motley little flock (12:32), doesn't appear to amount to much. This healing is a sign that it will take over the world, says Jesus. Just as a mustard seed grows into a tree, so the kingdom will grow (verses 18–19) – it will gain more and more adherents. More importantly, like yeast, the kingdom will work its way through the whole batch of dough that makes up this world (verses 20–21). Luke will tell the story in Acts.

Questions

1. Is there anything in the world more important than repentance? What exactly is repentance? Write a definition for a group of teenage Christians.
2. What evidence do we see around us in our communities that the kingdom of God like yeast is working its way through the world?

129

3. When our message causes division, even in families, how can we work for peace and reconciliation in the world?
4. Think of any non-Christian friends you have lost touch with. How can we make the most of the opportunities we have now to share the gospel?

Luke 13:22–35

Taking our place at the banquet

Religious people seem endlessly fascinated by the question of how many will be saved. Jesus warns us not to focus on that big picture, but rather to pay attention to whether we have repented and so are guaranteed our place at the table.

Luke reminds us that Jesus is travelling towards Jerusalem, making his way through the towns and villages of Galilee, teaching as he goes (verse 22).
He is gathering disciples and moulding them. So the question that kicks off the first part of this section is obvious enough (verses 23–30). Jesus' answer forces his hearers to think about their allegiance to him. When Pharisees warn him of Herod's murderous intent, the issue of allegiance to Jesus – this time the allegiance of Jerusalem at the heart of the nation – is still to the fore (verses 31–35).

The background to the first conversation in this section is the great banquet (Isaiah 25:6–9): who'll be there? There were a variety of views in first-century Israel (see on 14:1–26). The questioner clearly thought Jesus would have a view too.

As ever, Jesus isn't interested in tackling theoretical issues. He says the questioner should be striving to get in now because the door won't be open for long (verse 24). He then tells a parable about a householder throwing a banquet. Once the feast is due to start, the doors are closed and no-one arriving after that time will be able to get in (verse 25a). Potential diners will complain. But the host will say that their names aren't on the guest list (verse 25b).

Jesus clearly means us to see him as the host, and thus, as his answer unfolds, as the judge in whose hands hang the fate of everyone. The excluded guests protest that they've eaten with him before and listened to his teaching (verse 26). But again the host will say he doesn't know them. More than that, they are evildoers (verse 27).

Why so harsh a rebuttal? Jesus is stressing that turning up at the great banquet and claiming to have been at a party with him, or even to have heard his teaching, will not be enough. He has already made it clear that hearing the teaching must lead to doing it, otherwise it will have no effect (8:4–21; 11:28).

Notice that Jesus hasn't really answered the question yet. He's said who will be excluded and on what basis. He then turns to who will be coming to the banquet (verses 28–29). Abraham, the patriarchs and the prophets will, of course, be there (verse 28). But so will 'outsiders' (verse 29); countless people from all over the world will come to the banquet. But the people who expect to be there will be left out in the cold (verse 28c). Why will this happen? Because those who expect to be there, trusting in an accident of birth and a religion of exclusion as practised by the Pharisees, will find themselves overtaken by those who are there by virtue of the fact that they heard and obeyed the word of God through Jesus. These latecomers get preference (verse 30).

Before anyone can object, some Pharisees come with a warning for Jesus (verse 31). This should alert us to the fact that, though relations between Jesus and the religious elite are tense, they have not yet broken down altogether (cf. 14:1). Herod wants to kill Jesus (verse 31c). He should flee. This is Herod Antipas, who ruled Galilee in the north.

Jesus treats the messengers as people who have Herod's ear, indicating that he doesn't fully trust them (verse 32a)! He will continue his ministry – 'exorcism and healing' being

shorthand for all he does (4:18–19; 7:21–22) – according to
the timetable he has set himself (verse 32b; that's the force of
'today and tomorrow'). He has to do this because no
prophet can die outside Jerusalem, and Jerusalem is where
he's headed (verse 33b, cf. 22).

And suddenly the thought of his fate and the related fate
of that great city overwhelms him. He laments the coming
events. Jerusalem is the scene of the killing of God's
messengers in the past. It will be where he meets his death
(verses 33b–34a). But how sad it makes him! – not for
himself, but for the city. He longs for its people to repent
and come into the kingdom, to sit down at the great
banquet he's just been talking about (verses 25, 28–29). In a
wonderfully tender image, Jesus likens himself to a mother
hen gathering her chicks about her (verse 34).

But because she will not be gathered, she will be
scattered. She will be overwhelmed and destroyed (verse
35a, cf. 19:41–44; Jeremiah 12:1–7; 22:5). There is a sadness in
the quotation from Psalm 118 which ends the section:
Jerusalem could have welcomed Jesus with open arms as
the Lord's anointed. But in rejecting him now, they
condemn themselves to pronouncing him 'blessed' through
gritted teeth when he comes in judgment.

Questions

1. Is Jesus being fair to those who heard him but are refused
   entry to the banquet? What are the implications of this for
   our evangelism?
2. How could the hope of the great banquet inform our
   evangelism and communion services?
3. Jesus seems to imply that it is not right to ask 'theoretical'
   questions about our faith, like 'Will all non-believers be
   lost?' and 'Why does God allow disasters?' Are such
   questions wrong?
4. How often have we felt like weeping over the situation
   around us in our city or village? How can we turn our
   tears into action?

Luke 14:1–24

Look who's coming to dinner

**Jesus frequently ate with people who opposed his ministry.
Not that he was the easiest of dinner guests!**

The theme of the great banquet, which had featured prominently in the last section, dominates this one. Who will be on that guest list? Jesus was frequently invited to the glittering social functions of his day, though quite why is never really clear (verse 1b). But Jesus had a different guest list: he was calling people to a party for all the outcasts, the misfits, the sinners, the nobodies.

It was a Sabbath, and stories that begin 'One Sabbath' usually result in conflict. Jesus, as ever, meets it head-on. He challenges the Pharisees, and then when they baulk he heals the sick man – possibly one of the people who'd come to watch the gathering (see on 7:18–50). He then challenges the other guests to find fault through suggesting that the Sabbath should be a day for making people whole (verses 3, 5). But they're silent (verse 6).

Attention shifts to the jockeying for position and place at the party (verse 7). Perhaps many of the guests weren't really paying attention to the healing, because they were concerned to get the best places at the table. They certainly weren't concerned about a sick man in the crowd.

Jesus notices this and tells a stinging little parable (verses 8–11) containing common-sense advice. It is a gentle put-down of the social one-upmanship going on all around him. He is rather pointed with his host, telling him to invite not just his friends but also those who can't repay him: the poor, the outcast, the disabled, people like the man healed at the

133

beginning of the party (verses 12–14).

But people aren't paying attention, as is clear from the guest's comment in verse 15. And it sets the scene for another, more telling, parable which forms the climax of Luke's story (verses 16–24).

The dinner guest in verse 15 is referring to the great banquet that God invites his people to share, spoken of in Isaiah 25:6–10 (13:22–30). It seems that by the first century this had become one of the favoured images of the coming kingdom. Unfortunately, the various parties of first-century Judaism (see 'Sects and parties', p. 135) vied with one another over the guest list. The Pharisees thought only they and their kind would be invited. The Essenes believed only healthy Jews would be there: the poor, the disabled and the ritually unclean would be excluded.

What is clear is that this dinner guest, having jostled his way to a good seat at the table, was certain that he'd be on God's guest list. Jesus sees things very differently.

When a banquet was being thrown in the ancient world, the host would decide the size of beast to be barbecued on the basis of the number who'd responded to the invitation. Hence the sending of the servant to tell the guests that everything was ready (verse 17). The guests, however, at this stage insult their host by making palpably ludicrous excuses: a man claims he has paid money for a field that he hasn't seen (verse 18); another has bought oxen he hasn't tested – like buying a second-hand car over the phone without a test drive (19); another claims he'll be having sex while the party is on (verse 20).

No wonder the host is angry (verse 21). But he doesn't want his banquet to go to waste, so he sends his servant to bring in all those who'd never get an invitation to this kind of party: the poor, the outcast, those who couldn't repay the host's kindness. The element of compulsion contained in the phrase 'make them come in' (verse 23) does not mean that people have no choice in responding to the invitation. Rather, it is suggesting that the servant needs to stress that this amazing offer is genuine.

The parable is left unexplained to do its work on the

guests. For some it would have been water off a duck's back. Others it would have stung into furious opposition or weeping repentance. The message is clear: Jesus has come to call not the well-fed but the hungry. God's table is open to any and all who'll come, because the invitation has been sent to everyone. Some who've been invited might exclude themselves through their sniffy attitudes to others; but if we don't come when we're called, we'll miss out. There are no doggy bags from the great banquet.

Questions

1. Can we enjoy the banquet now, or only in the future kingdom? If now, what courses are being served, and how do we enjoy them? What excuses keep us away?
2. Is the gospel we proclaim to our friends and neighbours such good news that people can't believe it's for real? How do we convince them it is?
3. Are we always pushing ourselves forward, or shrinking into the background? How do we get the balance right?

Sects and parties

We meet a number of groups in the Gospel of Luke. Here's a guide to the key ones (see also 'The kingdom of God', p. 115).

▶ **The Pharisees**. Their name means 'separated ones', and they owe their origins to the time of the Maccabean revolt when some Jews were cosying up to Gentile culture and losing their distinctiveness. They were laymen, mainly concerned with purity and personal piety; hence their interest in ritual washing at mealtimes and their concern about eating with those who were 'unholy'. They took the law of God very seriously indeed and tried to apply it to every area of life; hence their penchant for adding interpretations to the law to help them stay on the straight and narrow.

They were generally popular with the mass of the people (largely because they weren't priests!) and they were open to new ideas: they believed such novel doctrines as the Holy Spirit, resurrection, the afterlife and angels.

▶ **The Teachers of the Law.** Closely allied to the Pharisees, these were experts in the law of Moses, and their role was to ensure that the law was correctly interpreted. They were also closely associated with the priesthood in Jerusalem; indeed, many of them may have been priests or Levites who did scribal study when they were not on duty in the temple.

▶ **The Sadduccees.** The priestly caste, they functioned as a sort of aristocracy within the Jewish state of Jesus' day. They were socially and theologically conservative, accepting only the first five books of the Bible as authoritative. Because they were allied with the political powers in the land, namely Herod and the Romans, they were powerful but unpopular. The council of elders (Sanhedrin) was made up largely of Sadduccees.

▶ **The Essenes.** This group doesn't appear in the Gospels, but its ideas were very important in first-century Israel. Little was known about them until their library was found in caves near the Dead Sea in the 1940s. They were based at Qumran, a monastery on the northern shore of the Dead Sea, but lived all over Israel. They were a protest movement against the Jerusalem priesthood, believing it to be irredeemably corrupt. At Qumran they pooled their possessions, lived by a strict community rule and longed that God would come and sweep away the Romans and the corrupt Jerusalem hierarchy and replace it with his direct rule.

▶ **The Zealots.** One of Jesus' disciples, Simon, had been a Zealot (Luke 6:15). Again, this group (or, better, collection of groups) doesn't appear in the Gospels. In any occupied land, resistance movements spring up. While the Pharisees and Essenes disliked Roman rule but were prepared to leave it to God to clear them out, the Zealots took direct action. From time to time through the first century, there were localized uprisings led by men who gathered groups around them, pitched them against the might of the legions and lost. Finally, in AD 66, they precipitated a rebellion that was widespread enough to require Rome itself to act. The result was the destruction of Jerusalem (AD 70) and the end of Israel as an independent territory for 1,900 years.

Luke 14:25-35

Weighing the cost of following Jesus

Following Jesus is not a spiritual option bolted on to an existing lifestyle. It is a complete shift of allegiance which demands that we leave all other loyalties and single-mindedly follow Jesus. Are we up for this?

 After the scene in the Pharisees' house, Jesus is once again on the road, drawing large crowds (verse 25). But now, instead of the stress being on Jesus teaching and performing wonderful deeds of healing

that amazed the crowd (e.g. 4:31, 40; 5:1), it is on the cost of being a follower of Jesus. Three times Jesus repeats the phrase 'cannot be my disciple' (verses 26b, 27b, 33b), as if his aim is to put off the casual enquirer. At the heart of the section are two mini-parables about not starting unless we're sure we'll see it through (verses 28–32).

Picking up his table-talk about who you invite for dinner (verses 12–13), Jesus tells his would-be followers that being a disciple means that family loyalties take second place. 'Hate' (verse 28) in this context is not about how we feel but who we take our lead from. In a culture where family ties were stronger and parental authority lasted longer into adulthood than in the modern western world, Jesus scandalously claims an allegiance that takes precedence over family.

We've already encountered this in his words to would-be followers as he started his journey to Jerusalem (9:59–62). Jesus is fleshing out those remarks here. He's already said that he had come to cause division in families (12:51–53); here he stresses that that division is caused by our choice to follow him.

But allegiance to Jesus is even more costly than loss of family relationships. It costs us our lives. We are to 'hate' our life (verse 26, recalling 9:23–25). We are to take up our cross (verse 27, cf. 9:23). Again this picks up on Jesus' dinner conversation. The trouble with the dinner guests was that they were too interested in the good things of life, in wealth and possessions, in status and position in society (verses 7–11, cf. 12:13–34). A disciple must 'hate' these things, leave them behind and strike out down the road behind a master who is going to Jerusalem to shoulder a cross.

He then tells two parables (verses 28–30, 31–32) which urge his hearers to weigh the cost before deciding to follow. Jesus was not like a modern evangelist, whipping up an emotional atmosphere in which people respond left, right and centre, sign on the dotted line and repent at leisure in the cold light of dawn. He doesn't want people to come after him who haven't first thought it through carefully.

The first parable concerns a tower-builder. Has he got the

money and materials to complete what he's started? If he hasn't, then he will be open to ridicule by his neighbours. To avoid this, the landowner needs to sit down and cost out his enterprise.

The second concerns a king on the brink of war. Even in the heat of indignation and national pride, will he not weigh up the consequences of going to battle against an enemy with twice the military muscle? To rush headlong into battle could result in humiliating defeat.

The punch-line to both parables is verse 33: are we prepared to give up everything to follow Jesus? For some, this will mean literally giving up everything (18:18–29). For others, such as Levi (5:28–29), it will mean putting what we have at Jesus' disposal. For all of us, it will mean that we no longer call the shots in our lives. We are bidding farewell (a possible meaning of the words translated 'give up everything') to our old life with its allegiances and joining Jesus on the road (verse 25, cf. 9:58).

A third parable drives the point home (verses 34–35a). Salt had two uses in Palestinian society, one as a flavouring and preserver of food, the other as a manure. It is absurd to think that salt could lose its saltiness. Likewise, it's absurd to think that we could be disciples and not abandon everything for Jesus.

Are we listening? The final phrase intentionally recalls the end of the parable of the sower (8:8): what kind of soil will these words of the Lord fall into?

Questions

1. How do we balance our responsibilities to our families with our discipleship? Is this possible?
2. How can we be sure that our evangelism gives people the space to weigh up the call of God and walk away from it or hang back until they're ready?
3. In a world of mortgages, jobs and credit-card bills, how can we abandon everything for Jesus? Should we be more radical? How can we do it?

Luke 15:1–32

The Father's heart for the lost

Jesus has shown that everyone is welcome in his band of disciples. Here he explains why. It is because of the passion of his Father to draw all people to himself.

Jesus' best-loved – and longest – parable (verses 11–31) was told in response to the Pharisees' attack on his dining companions (verse 2). In responding so  fully to his opponents' criticisms, Jesus gives us the fullest, and most sublime, insight into his Father's longing to gather the lost into his kingdom.

Despite his stern words about the cost of discipleship (14:25–35), people were still flocking to hear him. In terms of their stake in society, the tax collectors and other sinners (verse 1) were the 'poor' who'd always been the focus of Jesus' ministry (4:18–19; see 'Who are the poor?', p. 66). But to the Pharisees, these people were sinners whose lifestyles set them apart from God's kingdom people.

So Jesus tells three linked parables in which three items of increasing value go missing. In the first it's one sheep out of a hundred (verse 4); in the second, one coin out of ten (verse 8); in the third, one son out of two (verses 11–12). In all three, the central character searches for what is lost and rejoices by throwing a banquet of some kind when it is found.

In the first, the central character (rather pointedly in view of Jesus' audience) is a shepherd (verses 4–6) who diligently searches for a lost sheep, despite having ninety-nine safely at home in the fold. Having found it, he invites his friends to rejoice with him. 'Shepherd' was an Old Testament picture for Israel's leaders (Ezekiel 34:11–16). So Jesus is having a dig at his critics: they should be out looking for the lost, not smugly staying at home, blaming the strays for wandering off.

In the second, a woman (no less pointed, given the Pharisees' attitudes to women) searches for a coin. There is more stress in this parable on the diligence of the search; she lights a lamp in the daytime to illuminate the dingy corners of her windowless room (verse 8b). Again, having found the lost item, she celebrates with her neighbours.

Jesus draws the same point from both stories (verses 7, 10): that there is rejoicing in heaven when one sinner repents. The reference to the ninety-nine righteous (verse 7b) is ironic: Jesus surely intends his audience (the Pharisees) to repent.

The third parable, a complete family soap opera, concerns a father and his two sons. It is so famous and so loved that we may miss vital points if we do not read it carefully in the context in which Jesus told it.

The younger son insults his father by wishing him dead so he can have his inheritance now (verse 12a). Luke probably intended us to hear an echo of 12:13–21 and so identify the son as greedy and selfish. Certainly, Jesus does not minimize the extent of his sinfulness (verse 13, cf. 30). It's as if he's saying to his audience, 'Yes, I know these tax collectors and others are sinners ...'

That sinfulness is contrasted with the father's compassion. Having sunk as low as a young Jewish lad can (verses 15–16), he sets off for home. Whether this constituted repentance (it probably did, as Jesus repeats his speech 18–19, 21) is less important than the fact that all this time the father has been looking for his boy (verse 20a). The picture is of the man out at the gate of his estate, scanning the horizon.

Then, having espied his son, he runs (something a dignified father would never do in middle-eastern society) greets his son, restores him to his place in the family and throws a party (verses 22–24).

Enter the loyal elder brother (verse 25). In context, this figure surely represents the scribes and Pharisees, as the young son does the tax collectors and other sinners. He is livid. Having got the story of his younger brother's return from a servant, he refuses to join the party (verse 28a) – an echo of the Pharisees' refusal to eat with 'sinners', and an insult to his father.

Worse than that, having forced his father to leave the feast (something the host never did, once it was in full swing; 28b), he lays into him with words that indicate he doesn't want to be part of this family. He describes himself as a slave, not a son (verse 29), and disowns his brother with the words 'this son of yours' (verse 30a). The father urges his older son, who is a full member of the family as far as he is concerned (verse 31), to join the party because someone everyone thought was lost for ever has been found and restored to his rightful place (verse 32).

Again Luke doesn't tell us the outcome. We don't know what the elder brother did. We don't know how the Pharisees reacted. Jesus has laid out fully why his ministry is among the poor: because God longs for everyone to enjoy the benefits of his kingdom.

Questions

1. How do we feel when a sinner repents? How much are we prepared to change the way we do things in our church to accommodate new converts?
2. Put yourself in the shoes of the three main characters of the parable of the prodigal son (the father and the two sons). How do you feel as each scene unfolds? What do you think of the other characters?
3. Did the father act fairly towards his sons? Did he violate justice? How could a court have decided his case? What are the implications of this for our relationships with each other as Christians?

Luke 16:1–31

What's my money got to do with it?

Nothing is so contentious among religious people as money, because nothing shows so clearly where their hearts are. Here Jesus spells out in more detail his attitude to wealth: its use and its dangers.

While the Pharisees are digesting the three parables he's just told them, Jesus turns to teach his disciples (verse 1) more about the vexed issue of welcoming the poor and sharing their wealth with them. In another parable unique to Luke, Jesus warns his followers to use money rather than be used by it (verses 1–13). The eavesdropping Pharisees scoff at this teaching (verse 14). So Jesus contrasts their outward piety with their deceitful hearts (verse 15), telling them that for all their talk about obeying the law, they disregard what it says about helping the poor (verses 16–31).

The key to the parable of the unjust steward lies in the parallel between verses 4 and 9. The point Jesus is making – using a sleazy story from the world of finance, by which he warns his followers that money is inherently dishonest (verses 9–10) – is that we should use our money for promoting the values of the kingdom of God. More specifically, we should share what we have with the poor rather than hoarding our wealth for ourselves.

The manager in the story risks loss of status as well as of income (verses 2–3). So his actions are driven by the need to ensure that he will still be welcome at people's tables (verse 4). Effectively, he forces his master's hand by being generous in his name towards certain of his master's debtors (verses 5–7). Rather appallingly, his master commends his action (verse 8a). Even worse, Jesus does too (verses 8b–9), because it enables him to stress that what we do with our money expresses where our hearts are (cf. 12:31–34, especially 33; 14:12–14; e.g. Levi, 5:27–32, and Zacchaeus, 19:1–10).

From the parable, Jesus generalizes about our attitude to money (verses 10–13). We should see it, not as a neutral means of exchange, but as a power that seeks to control us (verse 13). So we should take control of it and make decisions about it based on the values of the kingdom (verses 10–12, cf. 12:31–34).

The Pharisees scoff at this because, as Luke tells us (as if he needed to!), they were lovers of money. Jesus scolds them with a searing condemnation of their hypocrisy (cf. 12:1), which pays huge attention to what people think of them but scant regard to how God sees their hearts (verse 15).

Then in a reversal of the norm, he accuses them of breaking the law (usually it's the other way around, e.g. 5:21–22; 6:2) by not welcoming and helping the poor (verses 16–18). The values of the kingdom don't contradict the law. Rather, they enact the law in its fullness, especially with regard to who's in and who's out of God's people. The phrase 'everyone is forcing his way in' (verse 16c) might be better rendered 'everyone is urged to enter it', because Jesus is contrasting the exclusivism of the Pharisees with the inclusiveness of God as demonstrated in the parables of 15:3–32.

The point about verse 18 is probably that a lot of money could be made, potentially by changing wives – and divorce was quite common in the first century. Many of the Pharisees were ready to interpret the law regarding divorce loosely for their own advantage, but were very strict in other areas. Jesus seeks consistency – and an example of how strictly Jesus enforces the law is seen in his saying on divorce (verse 18).

The law teaches care for the poor, as the parable that closes this section (verses 19–31) shows. It is a graphic commentary on Jesus' teaching in the Beatitudes (6:20–26, cf. 16:25). The rich man is fabulously wealthy (verse 19). The poor man is totally destitute (verses 20–21) – but notice he's the one with the name. Both die and their fortunes are reversed. Lazarus is comforted in the bosom of Abraham (verse 22) – an image of the great banquet (cf. 13:28–30) – while the rich man is tormented in the flames (verses 23–24). Having not lifted a finger to help Lazarus, the rich man now expects Lazarus to help him (verse 24), but Abraham says it's not possible (verses 25–26). So the rich man asks for Lazarus to be sent to warn his brothers; but Abraham says they have all the warning they need. Even someone rising from the dead won't persuade them (verses 27–31). Perhaps verse 31 is a wistful prediction that the Pharisees will never change, even after Jesus has been raised.

The point is that the law and prophets clearly spell out what God expects of his people concerning the poor. The hypocrisy of the Pharisees is that while heeding some of the law, they ignore important parts of it, including this key area (11:39–52). The disciples, however, should live by the values of the kingdom which uphold the law's emphasis on helping the poor, on sharing our possessions with those in need, and on graciously welcoming all, as God welcomes us.

Questions

1. Why does Jesus talk so much about money? Do we find it embarrassing? Awkward? Unspiritual?
2. What does this section teach us about how we should use our money? How can we help one another in our church to live up to this?
3. 'The parable of the rich man and Lazarus contradicts other Bible passages, teaching that we're saved by what we do, and not by what we believe.' Do you agree? Why or why not?

Luke 17:1–19

Serving out of gratitude

Have we learned the lessons the Pharisees failed to learn? Jesus draws out the implications of his teaching for his disciples and wonders if any of them yet has faith.

Again Jesus' attention shifts back to his disciples (verse 1). Have they taken to heart what he has been saying to the Pharisees? Here he spells out the  implications for their discipleship in terms of welcoming 'these little ones' (verses 1–3a) and sinners (verses 3b–4), being faithful to God (verses 5–6) and not using faith as a means of social climbing (verses 7–10). Then, with a reminder that all this is happening on the road, Jesus encounters a group of lepers and demonstrates the truth of his teaching through a miraculous sign that has particular impact on an 'outsider' (verses 11–17).

The tone of Jesus' words is more intimate than it's been for some time, indicating his concern that his followers should stay true to the kingdom. The world is full of pressures and temptations, 'things that cause people to sin' (verse 1). Perhaps Jesus has in mind persecution (cf. 6:22–23; 12:2ff.). He is clearly also thinking of the example that people of faith are to those around them (verse 2). Who are 'the little ones' he speaks of? From all that has led up to these words, it seems clear that this term refers to the poor – people like Lazarus in the last parable (16:19–31), the lost son (15:11–31) and the crippled, blind and lame (14:12–14).

To cause these little ones to stumble by excluding them from our community, by failing to share what we have with them, results in punishment: being dropped in the sea is preferable to what happened to the rich man (verse 2b, cf.

16:23–24). Little wonder that Jesus tells his followers: 'Watch yourselves' (verse 3a, cf. 12:1). We can't afford to be like the Pharisees in their indifference to the poor, he says.

But he goes on to tell us that we mustn't imitate the Pharisees in their attitude towards sinners either (verses 3b–4). They sniffily refuse to have anything to do with them (15:2). The followers of Jesus must, like their master, welcome sinners into their group and forgive them (verse 4) Sinners, of course, need to be told when they are wrong – hence the 'rebuke' (verse 3b). But mention of 'seven' indicates that forgiveness is an attitude rather than simply a one-off action (cf. 11:4).

The disciples' exclamation, 'Increase our faith!' (verse 5), indicates how difficult they find the prospect of living like this. 'Faith' here is 'faithfulness' to God's values: we need help to live this way. To encourage his followers, Jesus says we need only a grain of faith (verse 6: the mustard seed recalls the growing kingdom of 13:19) to live this way. The deeply rooted 'mulberry tree' (verse 6b) was proverbial of immovable objects. The question is: have the disciples yet got even this much faith?

Talk of faithfulness gives rise to talk of service (verses 7–10). We do not serve the kingdom to get ahead in the world – unlike the Pharisees. Jesus' parable (verses 7–9) suggests the absurd situation of a slave coming back from the field and being served by his master as a reward for his hard work. Similarly, we serve the interests of the kingdom not for any reward but because it is our duty as members of the kingdom (verse 10).

Reminding us that Jesus is on the road, Luke immediately shows us what serving that kingdom is about (verses 11–17). Notice that Jesus and his followers haven't got very far (verse 11b). This suggests that Jesus is taking his time because he wants to mould his disciples into true citizens of the kingdom, and clearly he still has some way to go.

Ten lepers meet him. The word translated 'leprosy' indicates that these individuals were suffering from various skin conditions (not just Hansen's disease, true leprosy) that rendered them ritually unclean and unable, because of fear of infection, to live at home in their villages. These were truly poor and unwelcome people. Notice that they kept their distance (verse 12b). They shouted their request from afar for fear of coming near and being rebuffed (verse 13).

Jesus' command to go and show themselves to the priest (verse 14a) was necessary because these men could not go home until the priest had confirmed that their illness had cleared up. As they go they are healed (verse 14b). At that point one of them returns to say thank you (verse 15).

Now Luke tells us that he was a Samaritan. You couldn't be much more of an outsider than that, and yet he is the only one who comes back to offer any gratitude to Jesus – something he acknowledges (verses 17–18) before assuring this Samaritan that his faith has made him well (verse 19).

The fact that he was a Samaritan raises the issue of which priest he would go to – one at Jerusalem or one at Gerizim (see 'Who were the Samaritans', p. 102). But perhaps his return offers a deeper insight: he sees Jesus, who cleansed him and welcomed him by faith into the community of the kingdom, as the 'priest' in whom God meets the world. It is no longer necessary to go to temples because through Jesus we are brought close to the Father. (This is the point Jesus himself will make forcefully on his entry into Jerusalem, 19:45–48.)

Questions

1. Sensitively discuss the damage that can be caused in church fellowship where there is lack of forgiveness. For reasons of personality and background, some people find it very hard to forgive others. How can they be helped?
2. How much do we actually engage in Christian service for selfish reasons?
3. Jesus is 'on the move' all during this part of Luke. How much is that a picture of Christian life? Is it helpful to think of it as a journey? What does that teach us?

Healing

Many of the stories Luke tells us about Jesus involve him bringing healing to people's lives. The word he used for 'salvation' and for 'healing' is the same in the Greek. So it is clear that his concern in these stories is to show how Jesus brought wholeness to people's lives through his ministry.

Look at the following stories and ask yourself:

▶ What did 'healing' mean for each of these people? (Think about not just the person healed but also others in the story, including the crowd.)

▶ What was the relationship (if any) between healing and faith?

▶ In what sense was each of these people 'saved' and 'whole' after his or her encounter with Jesus?

▶ What do the healings tell us about Jesus? Be specific.

5:12–16	A leper is given the chance to go home, be with his family and work at his trade.
5:17–26	A paralytic walks. His friends lend a hand; the Pharisees aren't sure.
7:11–17	A son raised and a widow given hope.
8:26–39	A demonized man is calmed.
8:40–56	A woman, a ruler, a little girl and a stunned crowd.
13:10–17	A woman is included in the family.
17:11–19	An outsider is given a new life.
18:35–42	A blind man sees. Do the onlookers get it?

In what ways should we seek to bring healing, wholeness and salvation to people today? Try to work out the ministry implications for your church.

Luke 17:20 – 18:8

Praying in the shadow of the kingdom

Speculation was rife about the 'when' and the 'where' of the kingdom. But Jesus is more concerned with its lifestyle and whether he'll find any of us living it when he comes again.

This section revolves around two questions concerning the kingdom (see 'The kingdom of God', p. 115) that arise out of Jesus' teaching. Pharisees ask,  'When is it coming?' (cf. verse 20) and disciples, 'Where will it be?' (cf. verse 37). In between, Jesus spells out the need to be ready (verses 26–30, the key verses in the section) because the kingdom is both here and still coming, a tension he spells out by using the phrases 'days of the Son of Man' (22, 26) and 'the Son of Man in his day' (verse 24; see 'The Son of Man', p. 191).

In response to the Pharisees' question (verse 20), Jesus replies that the kingdom is already among them (verse 21c; 'among' is better than 'within' here). Their expectation that the kingdom will come in some obviously visible form is wrong because it's based on the kingdom coming in a single cataclysmic act. No, says Jesus; it's worming its way in among you now. They should know this because of both his signs and his teaching (cf. 11:20).

Then, pre-empting the disciples' obvious question, 'So where is it?' (cf. verse 37), Jesus explains the tension between the 'now' and the 'not yet' of the kingdom. The disciples will long for the end to come (verse 22) because life is painful and hard. So they will be susceptible to those who claim that the kingdom is in a specific place (verse 23). But the day of the Son of the Man – the time when the kingdom of peace and joy comes in all its fullness – will be unmistakable (verse 24), so hang on. Before that can happen, however (just in case the disciples have forgotten) Jesus reiterates that he must suffer, be rejected and die (verse 25).

The 'days of the Son of Man' – the time now when the kingdom is already at work in the world through Jesus' and the disciples' ministries – will be like the days of Noah and Lot (verses 26–30). Normal life carries on and God's people should be involved in everyday affairs, eating and shopping, working and marrying.

But Jesus' followers mustn't be distracted from God and his kingdom's agenda by those normal, everyday activities. We must keep one eye on the sky. For as suddenly as the world was flooded or Sodom overwhelmed, so the Son of Man will come, and then his disciples must be prepared to drop everything and meet him. Their attachments to the things of this world must be loose and light (verse 31). They must not have a foot in both camps like Lot's wife (verse 32; Genesis 19:26), otherwise they will perish. So verse 33 recalls 9:23–26.

In that day the Son of Man will divide people as Simeon had said would happen (2:34–35), and as Jesus has said is happening already (12:52–53). In the midst of life, when the Son of Man comes, only those whose lives are oriented towards the kingdom will go to meet him (verses 34–35).

Given all that Jesus has said, the disciples' question (verse 37a) is as misguided as the Pharisees' (verse 20). Jesus says it will be as obvious as a kill in a desert (verse 37b). So, he says, rather than speculating on when and where these things will happen, we should be praying (18:1). And he drives the point home with a parable.

This short, simple story has two key points for his disciples – one concerning God, the other our faith. The parable concerns a judge who didn't give a fig for justice (verse 2) and a widow every bit as relentless in her quest for justice as a dog with a bone (verse 3). These two met head to head. The judge lost. He gave in, not in the interests of justice, but because he wanted a good night's sleep (verses 4–5).

The lesson concerning God comes out of the contrast Jesus' hearers draw between this awful judge and the God whom he's revealed to us as the loving Father (11:1–13). If even this judge gave justice, how much more quickly and fully will the gracious Father come to the aid of his children (7a, 8a)?

The lesson concerning our faith is drawn straight from the widow. She kept pressing her case to the judge. We ought to be continually pressing our concerns to God (verses 1, 7b). In the midst of the ordinary run of life with its routines and its ups and downs (17:26–35), God's kingdom people should be praying. In the midst of the pain and uncertainty of opposition and persecution (17:22–25), God's kingdom people should be praying.

Having laid out the complex picture of the coming of the kingdom, both now and in the future, Jesus ends by asking a simple, straight question that each of his disciples has to answer. When the Son of Man comes (i.e. on that great day when he comes as judge), will he find faith on the earth? Will he find a band of loyal people living according to his values in the light of his coming?

Questions

1. What does this section tell about the second coming of Jesus?
2. In what ways are we like the widow in our prayer lives? How can we learn to be like her?
3. How can we keep from despairing when we look at what's happening in the world around us? What help is the tension between the 'now' and 'not yet' of the kingdom? And what help is the story of Lot and his wife?

The righteousness of the kingdom

We can enter the kingdom only if we receive it as a gift. Our piety, position, wealth, wisdom or status counts for nothing. Each one of us has to come as an empty-handed child to our Father.

Jesus is nearing Jerusalem. The next geographical marker will tell us that he has less than twenty miles to go (verse 35). The final part of the travel narrative opens and closes with a parable unique to Luke (18:9–14; 19:11–27). In between, the author tells us about three significant meetings Jesus had with possible disciples. It's time for decisions: are we a part of the kingdom being proclaimed by Jesus or not? Time is short.

The opening parable in this section is set in the temple at the time of the evening sacrifice. We assume that Jesus is aiming this one at the Pharisees (verse 9), but the disciples need to pay attention too in view of their track record (9:46–50), not to mention their current behaviour (verses 35; 22:24–28).

Two men go up to pray, a Pharisee and a tax collector (verse 10). We imagine Jesus' audience at this point mentally marking the Pharisee down as a good pray-er and wondering what the tax collector was doing there at all. And true to form the Pharisee demonstrates his wonderful oratory (verses 11–12). He is very holy, keeps himself pure, fasts and avoids the company of sinners like the tax man. There is genuine thankfulness in his words. The audience would be swooning with admiration. But note that Jesus tells us he was praying 'about' or even 'to' himself (verse 11a).

The tax collector keeps his distance (verse 13a). He gazes at the floor, beats his breast and longs for his sins to be carried away with the evening sacrifice along with those of the righteous who have come (verse 13b).

Then comes the shocker. Jesus says this man, not the pious Pharisee, is right with God (verse 14a). Why? Because he, unlike the Pharisee, humbles himself before God, recognizes he has nothing to bring to the party and relies totally on God's grace (14b).

As he tells this story, young mothers are bringing their babies for Jesus to bless (verse 15). The disciples, thinking that the kingdom is only for sophisticated insiders like themselves, try to keep them away. Jesus rebukes them (verses 16–17). The kingdom, he tells them, is made up of people who come like children: those who recognize that they have no status before God, nothing to bargain with before heaven's throne – like the tax collector in the parable.

Among the young mums is a rich man (verse 18), a ruler (probably in a synagogue). You can imagine the crowd parting to let him approach Jesus. If anyone is worthy of a place at the table for the great banquet, it is this man. But Jesus is not impressed by outward appearance or by the man's ingratiating address of 'Good teacher'. Jesus isn't playing that status game: the same rules apply to everyone (verse 19). Eternal life (verse 18b) is about embracing the values of the kingdom, which include the law (verse 20, cf. 16:16–18). The young man is fastidious in observing the law (verse 21).

Now comes the bombshell. This man lacks one thing (22a). What could this wealthy, powerful man possibly be lacking? He needs to sell what he has, share it with the poor, and follow Jesus. If he does this, he'll have treasure in heaven (12:31–34). He can't do it (verse 23).

In asking the young man to give up his wealth, Jesus is asking him to become like a child (verse 17), someone who has no obvious status to rely on, no wealth to impress us. What he lacks is the humility to receive eternal life as a gift of grace from God (verse 14).

To the gasping crowd – for surely, they think, this man

out of all of them is a dead cert for the kingdom – Jesus says that the rich and powerful will find it especially difficult to enter. Indeed, it will be as hard for them to get in as it is to get the family pet through a needle's eye (verses 24a–25). Jesus is not saying it's hard; he's saying it's impossible.

No wonder the crowd exclaims, 'Who then can be saved?' (verse 26). Jesus' reply is that entering the kingdom is a gift – but you have to put down what you're holding (in this man's case his wealth, status and position) in order to take it (verse 27).

Peter's statement sounds a little smug (verse 28). But Jesus hears in it the insecurity of one who wonders if he has sacrificed enough, and moves to reassure him, in words reminiscent of those promises he's made before, that God will supply their every need if they follow him and live for his kingdom (verses 29–30, cf. 11:1–13; 12:22–34).

Questions

1. What's wrong with the way the Pharisee prays? What's right about the way the tax collector prays?
2. If the rich and powerful find it so hard to enter the kingdom, why is the church so full of the middle-class, the prosperous, the well-heeled and respectable?
3. What things have we received in this life as a result of following Jesus?

Luke 18:31–43

Seeing the cost of the kingdom

The disciples can't see what Jesus is about. A blind man sees clearly that he is the Son of David. Getting to grips with the kingdom is a matter of faith. Have we seen it?

One of the key elements of Jesus' ministry according to his manifesto was to bring recovery of sight to the blind (4:18–19). Luke has not told us a story of that happening yet. He does so here in a section which also tells us about the blindness of those who should by now have been able to see (in the metaphorical sense, verses 31–34), in contrast to the blind man who 'saw' clearly who Jesus was, even when he was blind (verses 35–43).

As the crowd digested the significance of the encounter between Jesus and the ruler, he takes his disciples to one side to remind them of the reason for their journey (verse 31a). From how they've reacted (verse 15) and what they've said (verses 26–28), it's clear that even the twelve are struggling to grasp what it's all about.

Jesus talks about his destiny in the fullest and starkest language yet (verses 31b–32). His rejection by the leaders of his people will result in his humiliation at the hands of the Romans (the Gentiles, verse 32). Crucifixion was an awful punishment inflicted by a cruel and powerful empire on its enemies. Its intention was not just to kill its victim but to deter others from following in their footsteps by making that death as public and degrading as possible.

Notice that Jesus says this will happen to the 'Son of Man' (verse 31b; see p. 191). This has always been Jesus' favourite term for himself, but he has been using it more frequently as they have neared Jerusalem (e.g. 17:20ff.). It is clearly intended to demonstrate to his followers that his death is more than just a bloody end to a powerful but misunderstood ministry. Because the vision of the Son of Man in Daniel 7:13–14 is of a figure ascending to God to receive authority, Jesus hopes that his disciples will see that the coming of the kingdom and his death are intimately linked. This is reinforced by his clear prediction that he will rise again (verse 33).

But Luke tells us (in three phrases that amount to the same thing) that the disciples just don't see it (verse 34). They are blind to what Jesus is saying to them – partly through their own lack of understanding, partly because what Jesus is saying doesn't match their expectations of what will happen to the Messiah (see the comments on 9:18–27) and partly because God has to reveal the truth of it to the eyes of faith.

Immediately the disciples receive a lesson in how this happens – assuming they're looking. Approaching Jericho, they encounter a blind man (verse 35). He is begging because he has no other way of supporting himself. It almost certainly indicates that he has no family, or that his family is so poor that they can't support a mouth that isn't contributing to the family's income. He doesn't even have a name. Truly, he is a poor man.

A crowd is gathering – not the same crowd that was following Jesus, but locals who have come out to see the rabbi with a reputation from up north in Galilee. They tell the blind man to be quiet. They obviously think (based on their experience of the Pharisees, no doubt) that great religious teachers haven't time for the likes of blind beggars (verse 39).

Notice that twice the blind man calls Jesus 'Son of David' (verses 38, 39b). He 'sees' that Jesus was something special, more than just another wonder-working teacher; he 'sees' he is the promised king, come to set his people free. It is a frequent occurrence in Luke that those on the margins of the people of God – the poor, the sick, outsiders – grasp more quickly than those at the centre of things (including the disciples) who Jesus is (e.g. a Gentile centurion, 7:1–10; a nameless sinner from the city, 7:36–50; a Samaritan leper, 17:11–19).

Jesus hears him calling and stops (verse 40). It is a lovely picture of the gentleness and grace of the Son of David. He is the long-expected king on his way to meet his destiny in Jerusalem. He is concerned that his courtiers (the disciples) still haven't grasped what his mission is about. Yet he is able to stop for a nameless blind man.

Having asked him what he wants (verse 41), he tells him his faith has made him well (verse 42). With his sight restored, he and the crowd follow Jesus, praising God.

He has 'seen' who Jesus is, and through his faith has received his sight. The disciples have seen all that Jesus has been doing and yet still don't seem to have the faith to 'see' what Jesus is really about, and to recognize him, as the blind man has done, as 'Son of David'. They are still fulfilling Isaiah's prophecy, despite being given insight into the secrets of the kingdom (8:9–10). But Jesus hasn't given up on them.

Questions

___

1. What had the blind man seen that the disciples hadn't?
2. How can we help people who've heard the story of Jesus countless times to hear it again in such a way that they 'see' it for the first time?
3. What do the two titles 'Son of Man' and 'Son of David' tell us about Jesus? What do they tell us about how we should respond to him?

Luke 19:1–10

Paying the price of the kingdom

Zacchaeus came looking for Jesus in the hope of finding acceptance. Jesus was already looking for Zacchaeus in order to welcome him into the kingdom. Here's the wonderful story of the day they met.

 Jesus doesn't look as if he intends to stop in Jericho (verse 1). Yet it's in this town that he has one of the most significant encounters of his journey. It is his last prior to his arrival in Jerusalem, and it enables Luke to end the travel narrative on a high note. This meeting picks up the themes of 'seeing' and 'wealth' from the previous sections, and gives us a rich picture of a 'poor' man entering the kingdom through his encounter with Jesus.

In a wonderfully told tale, Luke tells about two men who were 'looking', about how the crowd judges people by outward appearances and how Jesus brings real change into people's lives.

Jesus, we know, is steadfastly heading towards Jerusalem. The closer he gets the more focused he becomes on his goal (18:31–33). So it's not surprising that he passes through Jericho (verse 1). There's a sense of urgency in Luke's narration.

But there's a man in Jericho keen to meet Jesus. Zacchaeus is a wealthy chief tax collector (verse 2). Like Levi (see on 5:27 – 6:16), he is unpopular – and for good reason. As a chief tax collector, he is probably responsible for collecting the taxes on behalf of Rome for a whole area. A number of people like Levi work for him. He probably runs the local tax system, much as modern-day Mafiosi run protection rackets. Tax demands are accompanied by the threat of violence, however extortionate they seem.

But Zacchaeus wants to see Jesus (verse 3). Perhaps he's heard about him from other tax collectors, who have told him how this teacher doesn't reject his kind; in fact, he welcomes them so much that he is known as a friend of tax collectors and sinners. Perhaps he longs for forgiveness, a relationship with God and sense of belonging to his people denied him by the good religious folk of his day, who have him written off as an irredeemable sinner.

But he is short (verse 3b). So we have this wonderful picture of a beautifully dressed, wealthy man wedged in a tree trying to get a good look at a scruffy teacher from Nazareth who's been on the road for weeks (verse 4). Zacchaeus is lacking stature in another sense of course; he is an outsider, like the blind man, the children, the tax man and the widow of chapter 18 – one of the poor to whom Jesus is bringing good news (4:18–19). Perhaps this is another reason he can't get through the crowd – they hate him (verse 7).

When Jesus arrives beneath the spot where Zacchaeus is wedged, an amazing thing happens. He looks up and tells the tax man to come down, because he 'must stay' with him today (5b). The word translated 'must' is one that Luke uses only to describe divine necessity. Jesus' dinner with Zacchaeus is ordained by God for a reason. So obviously Jesus hadn't intended to pass through Jericho; he'd always been going to a meeting with the local tax man.

Naturally Zacchaeus is bowled over and welcomes him gladly into his home (verse 6). The crowd is stunned. Of all the people to stay with on a flying visit to Jericho, this tax collector is the worst. He is a sinner (verse 7).

Between verses 7 and 8, a whole conversation takes place that Luke doesn't tell us about. When Zacchaeus speaks, he is a changed man. He shows this through giving half his possessions to the poor and repaying fourfold those he's defrauded (verse 8). Why doesn't he give everything, as Jesus had demanded of the rich man (18:22)? Because, like Levi, what matters is that people put what they have at

Jesus' disposal and show this by sharing with the poor (5:27–32; 11:41; 12:32–34; 14:12–14; 16:1–31).

As a result of Zacchaeus' action, Jesus declares that salvation has come. This tax man, no less than anyone in the crowd, is a child of Abraham (verse 9, cf. 13:16). Because of his faith, seen in his practical good works (showing solidarity with the poor), this man is part of the people to whom God made his promise of salvation all those years ago.

Then Jesus tells us that the reason Zacchaeus was found was not that he was looking for Jesus, but that Jesus was looking for him (verse 10). This verse is a wonderful summary of Jesus' whole ministry: he'd come to look for what had been lost (cf. 15:1–32) and to restore it to its rightful place in the kingdom of God.

Questions

1. Is there a Zacchaeus in your neighbourhood? What would happen if he turned up at church?
2. Are we willing to scandalize public opinion for the sake of the gospel? How?
3. Did Zacchaeus buy his way into the kingdom? What does his action tell us about the kingdom and money?

Luke 19:11–27

Rejecting or welcoming the king

Hailing Jesus as king is one thing. But living under his rule is another. Jesus is looking for subjects who will do the work he did of taking good news to the poor.

The key to understanding this parable lies in the careful way Luke sets it up. The audience for it is the crowd that has seen Zacchaeus welcomed into the  kingdom (verse 11a). That crowd will inevitably have included disciples, Pharisees and assorted onlookers. Jesus is near Jerusalem, the place of destiny (verse 11b; cf. 9:31, 51, 53; 13:22, 33–34; 17:11; 18:31–34). And people think the kingdom is going to appear at once (verse 11c). Luke has been stressing that the kingdom is both present and coming (see 'The kingdom of God', p. 115), so the parable is concerned directly with that question.

In many ways it is a succinct summary of the key issue of the travel narrative: will we accept or reject Jesus as king? More than that, will we serve this king by working to promote his kingdom? As in the parable in 12:35ff., Jesus has an eye on both his first coming, which took the religious leaders of his day by surprise, and his second, which it's to be hoped won't catch us on the hop (see on 12:22–48).

This parable looks back over Jesus' ministry. Jesus was proclaimed king at his baptism. Many have acknowledged that kingship, not least the blind man at the gates of Jericho where this story is being told (18:35–43). Many have rejected his claim, namely the Pharisees. It also looks forward: Jesus is about to be proclaimed king by the people (verses 28ff.), and just as firmly rejected by their leaders, before being ratified by God (22:66–71; Acts 2:36).

The action of the parable is drawn from Israel's recent history. In 4 BC Archelaus, son of Herod the Great, went to Caesar to have his kingship over Judea ratified. No sooner had he left than a delegation of Judeans hot-footed it to Rome to object (cf. verse 14). He was eventually deposed and banished in AD 6. Some in Jesus' audience would have taken sides in that fairly recent event. Of course, Jesus is inviting his audience to take sides again: will they have *him* as king or not?

The details of the parable are fairly straightforward. The king goes off to be ratified (not an uncommon event in the Roman Empire) and leaves his servants in charge of business back home. They would be expected to run his affairs efficiently and effectively in his absence and then to give an account of themselves when the king returned (verses 13–15).

The fact that the king gives his servants *money* recalls some key parts of Jesus' teaching during his journey to Jerusalem (viz. 12:22–34 as well as 35ff.; 16:1–31). The issue when he calls those servants to account is whether they have been trustworthy with what was entrusted to them (directly recalling 16:10–12).

A mina was about three months' wages for a labourer, so no-one had been given a trifling sum. The first servant had made a 1,000% return on his cash (verse 16), the second 500% (verse 18). In the light of chapter 16, it would not be unreasonable to suggest that Jesus expects us to apply this to the way we use our money to promote the values of the kingdom – namely, to make friends, win subjects (16:9) – though a wider application to the use of all the gifts God has given us for the work of the kingdom is not out of the question.

The reward for the first two servants is that they are to be given more responsibility (cf. 16:10). The word translated 'earned' (verse 18) recalls the fruitfulness that Jesus looks for in those who respond to his word (it's used in 6:46; 8:19–21). Jesus is clearly envisaging that those who accept him as king will work, as he has done, to extend the reach of his kingdom to more and more people. Hence the reward is responsibility for the governance of cities.

The third servant has done nothing with his money and justifies his inaction by claiming that the king is a harsh man who rules unjustly (verses 20–21). Perhaps we are meant to see him as someone who was initially attracted to King Jesus but then decided he was a fraud and sided with those who rejected him (Judas?). The king condemns him with his own words by suggesting that just by banking the cash, he'd have got some interest (something forbidden to Jews, of course). But the man is not punished; he only loses his mina (verse 24).

The parable ends with a savage judgment on those who had opposed the king's rule (verses 26–27). Rejecting the king has fearful consequences.

The challenge of the parable to us is that accepting Jesus as king is not just about our words (13:22–27), but also about our actions – as in the case of Zacchaeus (19:8; cf. 8:4–15; 11:28). All through the travel narrative Jesus has been urging his disciples to see that following him is about doing what he does – bringing good news to the poor in word and deed. Here, before the final confrontation with the powers that be when his kingship will be decisively rejected, Jesus reminds us of that lesson one last time.

Questions

1. Have you ever conducted a 'gifts audit'? It's a way of deciding, in fellowship and consultation with others, which 'gifts' each of us has to use for the King. Why not do this in your group?
2. In what ways do you think that verse 22 is an accurate, true picture of God?
3. Verse 24 seems very unfair; see the reaction in the next verse. Why does God treat people so unequally?

Gifts

Jesus has a lot to say about how we use what we've been given. We tend to drive a wedge between natural talents and spiritual gifts (as we read about them in Paul's letters, for instance in 1 Corinthians 12). But this doesn't do justice to the particular 'angle' on gifts that we find in Luke's Gospel.

In a sense 12:48 (repeated in 19:26) is the key text: what we have been given, we are expected to use.

▶ What have we been 'given' here?

▶ How are we supposed to use it?

Wrestle with this text for a while and tease out what it's saying about your life as a disciple. Then look at the following texts:

1:73–74	The gift of serving God without fear. What does this mean?
8:9–10	We've been given the secrets of the kingdom. What are they?
8:16–18	We will not understand if we don't listen. How is listening related to being given things?
10:19	How do we experience and exercise the authority Jesus speaks of here?
12:31 (22–34)	What are the things we'll be given if we seek the kingdom? How will we receive them?
16:10–12	In what sense have we been given money? What is its relationship to the 'true riches' spoken of here?
18:29 (18–30)	Where and when do we receive these things?

19:11–27   What does this story tell us we should be
              doing with what God gives us? What will
              happen if we do it?

THE JOURNEY UP:
The passion narrative

Luke 19:28 – 24:53

Stop and look

We have reached the climax of Luke's tale. It is important that we come to these chapters fresh. Our problem is that we know these stories so well and could easily miss the subtle nuances of Luke's telling of them.

Beginning with Jesus' triumphant entry into Jerusalem for his final confrontation with the Jewish authorities (a confrontation we know has been coming since 6:11) and ending with Jesus' triumphant departure from the Mount of Olives to heaven, this section takes us on an emotional roller-coaster ride.

We are buoyed by the reception the Jerusalem crowd gives to Jesus and thrilled by his outsmarting of the scribes and priests in various set-piece disputes. Then we are alarmed by the willingness of Judas to betray his master, moved to tears by the pathos of the last meal Jesus shared with his friends, angered by the blindness of his judges at Jesus' trial and numbed with pain at the crucifixion, before exploding with an uncomprehending joy at his resurrection.

Luke tells the story carefully, showing us, as he did in the birth narratives, how what is happening is fulfilling Scripture. God is working to a plan, and mysteriously that plan involves the cutting down of the gentlest, most loving man ever to have walked the planet. The plan also involves breaking the power of the forces of darkness through the innocent suffering and vindication of the Chosen One.

Read these words prayerfully; you are walking on holy ground indeed.

Welcoming the king

The crowd hail him as king. The power-brokers try to shut him up. Whose side are we on as Jesus comes to claim his crown?

In four movements, Luke brings Jesus from Jericho, not far from Jerusalem, into the temple at the heart of Israel's capital city. He tells us how Jesus set up his entry into the city (verses 28–34), how he rode into Jerusalem to the acclamation of his followers (verses 35–40), how he wept over the city and its people (verses 41–44), and how he prepared the temple to receive his teaching (verses 45–48).

Luke tells us Jesus travelled through Bethphage and Bethany and paused at the Mount of Olives (verses 28–29). Notice how much detail Luke gives us in an effort to slow the pace of the story and heighten the tension.

It appears that Jesus has set up his entry into the city with some care. He sends two disciples off to a prearranged meeting to obtain a colt that hasn't yet been ridden (verse 30). Having walked all the way from Galilee, he will ride the last hundred yards or so in a self-conscious fulfilment of prophecy (Zechariah 9:9) and overt declaration of who he is. So the disciples are sent with a password and find everything as Jesus said it would be (verses 31–34).

Spreading their coats on the animal, the disciples sit their king on the colt and set off towards the city singing and shouting. They quote Psalm 118:26 (verse 38a), but put the word 'king' where the original just has 'he', so that the people of Jerusalem will be in no doubt that it is *their* king who is coming. The reference to 'peace' (verse 38b) is an echo of Zechariah 9:9–10 – a sign that Jesus comes not as a warrior to defeat his enemies but as a gentle king to woo them over – and of the word of the angels in 2:14. The fact that it is in heaven rather than on earth is a sign that the king has not yet been accepted by his people. Is it now too late?

The Pharisees are aghast, appealing to Jesus to stop the singing (verse 39). This is a demonstration that will worry the Romans watching from the Antonia Fortress next to the temple. More than that, they do not believe it is true, and expect Jesus to agree with them. He doesn't. Not only does he accept the crowd's adulation and affirmation of his kingship; he says that if the crowd were silent, you'd hear the very stones of the city singing – as if the brickwork knew better than its inhabitants who was coming (verse 40).

Jesus then breaks down and weeps over the city. He knows what awaits him on the other side of the gates (9:22, 43b–44; 13:34–35; 17:25; 18:31–34). He takes up the cry for peace in the disciples' song (42, cf. 38b) and laments that the people don't know how to obtain it. They assume that peace is only the absence of war – something the elders can hang on to providing they keep the mob and the extremists in check. The peace Jesus brings is the wholeness of relationship and welfare for all the people that comes from enjoying the rule of God, not the rule of Rome.

Because they refuse this, they will lose their grip on what fragile peace they have, and the whole volatile situation will blow up in their faces, leaving them with no city and eventually no nation (verse 43). Worse than that, there will be no temple. When the armies come and destroy the city, they will raise to the ground that symbol of all that the people hold dear and trust in (verse 44a) – all because they failed to recognize the day when God came to town (verse 44b).

And with that bold statement still being digested by those around him, Jesus sweeps into the temple and cleanses it. Luke's account is short and fast. Jesus drives out the traders and declares that the temple ought to be a place for praying (verses 45–46). What is he doing?

According to Luke, Jesus has not been in the temple since

he was twelve (2:40–50). Having listened then (as well as asking questions), this time he is speaking by both his words and his actions.

His words suggest that if the temple had been a house of prayer, the people, especially the leaders, would have known who Jesus was. This is because in Luke there is a close link between praying and revelation (verse 46a; cf. 3:21–22; 4:42–44; 9:18–20; 10:21–22). His actions strike at the heart of the economic power of the Jerusalem leaders in controlling the animals for sacrifice and the cash for the temple tax. He describes this power as banditry (verse 46b, cf. Jeremiah 7:3–20).

Not surprisingly, those leaders wanted to silence him (verse 47) – permanently. Note that we have said goodbye to the Pharisees; we left them at the gates of the city (verse 39) to be replaced by their allies the teachers of the law and the real power holders, the chief priests. But, despite the fact that he taught openly in the temple every day, they couldn't touch him, because the people – that is, both Jesus' travelling companions and the ordinary folk of Jerusalem, to whom Jesus' teaching was exciting and new – 'hung on his words' (verse 48).

The scene is set for the final showdown.

Questions

1. What are the main points of contrast between Jesus' claim to Israel's crown and the usual bid for power by politicians and generals?
2. Does Jesus' prediction of Jerusalem's destruction mean that he accepts that war and conflict are part of the world order and his people should just go along with this?
3. What was Jesus doing in the temple? What lessons are there for our churches? Remember that 'selling' took place to enable visitors to Jerusalem to obtain the special shekels they needed in order to buy things for the feast. Why did Jesus object to this?

Luke 20:1-26

Questioning the king

Jesus has challenged the authority of the Jerusalem leaders in the heart of their power base, the temple. What gives him the right?

It's traditional to think that Jesus was in Jerusalem for a week. Luke doesn't actually tell us how long he spent teaching in the temple. What he gives us  instead is a flavour of it. And in this section he focuses on the clash between the claimant to Israel's throne and the existing Jerusalem leadership.

For emphasis, Luke tells us twice that these encounters about authority take place in the temple (19:47; 20:1). Jesus' audience is 'the people', who act as a buffer between Jesus and the Jewish leaders (19:47, 48; 20:1, 9, 16b). The three parts of this section are each concerned with the authority of Jesus against that of the leaders in Jerusalem. First, they ask him outright where he gets his authority from (verses 1–8). Then he tells a parable about how they have abused their authority and will be held accountable by God (verses 9–19). Finally, they try to trap him into challenging Rome's authority (verses 20–26).

The whole Jerusalem establishment is represented in the first challenge – priests, teachers and members of the council (verse 1b). 'These things' (verse 2a) refers both to Jesus' teaching and to the manner of his entry into the city and action in cleansing the temple (see on 19:28–48). His questioners base their authority on birth, position, education and wealth. By what right does Jesus challenge it?

Jesus answers their question with a question. To answer directly would be to play into their hands and give them a pretext on which to have him arrested. All through this section, Jesus opens up their motives to the scrutiny of the people and allows them to assess who's right. His question about John is a perfect example of this.

But Jesus isn't just being clever. John prepared the way for Jesus (1:16–17, 32–35, 68–76; 3:16), so to accept John as a prophet, as the people did (verse 6b), means they'd have to accept Jesus as the rightful king. To reject John openly not only risks the wrath of the crowd (verse 6a), but shows the leaders up to be out of step with God (cf. 7:29–30).

Their answer is a cop-out (verse 7). Jesus' reply (verse 8) paves the way for the devastating parable of the tenants, in which Jesus claims the unique authority of the vineyard owner's son and writes off the Jerusalem leadership as unfruitful tenants (cf. 8:4–15).

The background to the parable is Isaiah 5:1–7. In it Jesus tells the people (verse 9a) the sorry history of Israel: planted by God but so badly managed that none of the fruit the owner expected came his way. Prophets and messengers were shamefully treated, and finally his son was sent and killed (verses 9–15a). Thus far Jesus follows Isaiah's text. But then he departs from it. For whereas Isaiah goes on to speak of judgment against the vineyard, Israel (Isaiah 5:5–7), Jesus goes on to speak about judgment against the vineyard's managers, Israel's leaders (verses 15b–16a).

The people are stunned (verse 16b). The leaders are livid (verse 19). Jesus has answered their question (verse 2) by claiming to be the king sent by God: no-one can have a greater authority. Of course, Jesus is here saying that these leaders will get their way; he will be killed (verse 17). But the consequences for them will be catastrophic (verse 18, cf. 21:5–28).

Their challenge now shifts. If Jesus is claiming an authority greater than theirs, is he claiming an authority greater than Rome's? Agents are recruited to try to get Jesus to utter treason against the governor, Rome's representative in Jerusalem (verse 20). Jesus, of course, knows he is being set up (verse 23) – not hard to spot, given the mealy-mouthed, ingratiating nature of their approach (verse 21).

Their question (verse 22) is about the 'head tax' that Rome levied on every male subject and which was the reason for the census where Jesus' story begins (2:1–7). This tax (also known as 'tribute') was charged at the rate of one denarius (a day's wage for a labourer). It wasn't especially onerous, but to a Jew it represented the fact that they weren't masters in their own land.

The spies hope either that Jesus will utter treason and so get arrested by the Romans, or that he'll tell people to pay up and thus lose the sympathy of the crowd, so that the elders can lay their hands on him. Either way Jesus is bound to lose. Or so they think.

He asks for a coin. They give him one and immediately they are sunk. They hold the hated coinage because they – or at least their masters, the Sanhedrin – collect the tax on behalf of Rome. They are part of the machinery of tyranny defending the temple by serving the idolatrous Romans.

Jesus' answer (verse 25b) is another take on his saying about serving two masters (16:13). Rome, like wealth, possessions and family ties, finds its rightful place in the lives of God's people only once the issue of primary loyalty has been settled. The Jerusalem leaders, false tenants, appeared to give their primary loyalty to Rome, not God. To whom do we give ours?

Questions

1. Look again at how Jesus replies in verses 3–4, 23–24. Have you ever had to face (even mildly) hostile questioning about your faith? How did you respond? How can we prepare ourselves for this?
2. Jesus is the rejected son (verse 15). What does this teach us about how to combat the world's wickedness?
3. How can we ensure that Christian leaders don't suffer the same fate as Israel's leaders according to the parable of the tenants?

Luke 20:27 – 21:4

Recognizing the king

God has revealed in the Bible how he wants his people to live. But unless we interpret his Word correctly and live by it, we turn it into a system that oppresses people.

Jesus has been challenged over whether his authority is greater than that of the Jerusalem leaders or the Romans. In this section the challenge is even more fundamental: what is his authority in relation to the Scriptures? First he is asked outright by the Sadducees (verses 27–40). Then he asks about the meaning of another text (verses 41–44). Finally, he asserts his right to interpret Scripture authoritatively by showing how his opponents have failed to take seriously what those Scriptures say about money, social status and the values of God's kingdom (20:41 – 21:4).

The Sadducees were allied to the group that has been challenging Jesus up till now. They were members of the ruling elite in Jerusalem, wealthy and conservative. Luke tells us they didn't believe in the resurrection, unlike the scribes and Pharisees (verse 27). They also accepted only the first five books of the Old Testament as authoritative Scripture, and failed to find the resurrection taught here. So superficially, their encounter with Jesus centres on a live doctrinal dispute: do you believe in the resurrection? In fact, the underlying issue is the more important one: who has authority to interpret Scripture?

The Sadducees set Jesus a patently ludicrous problem (verses 29–32). Its starting-point is so-called levirate marriage (verse 28, cf. Deuteronomy 25:5; Genesis 38:6–11; Ruth 3:9 – 4:10). The Sadducees believed that people lived on through their descendants, not in any kind of afterlife. Resurrection was not necessary, they thought.

Jesus answers them by contrasting life in the age to come with that of this age (verses 34–36), and then by showing that Moses believed in resurrection (37–38). In the age to come we'll be like the angels only in as much as we won't die (verse 36). Whether or not there'll be marriage really depends on whether Jesus is saying that marriage belongs only to this age, or that only the use by men of women as chattels in marriage to produce progeny belongs to this age (verses 34–35).

If the latter, then Jesus is attacking the Sadducean acceptance of the treatment of women as little more than objects to bear children. Such an attack makes sense in view of what comes later (20:45 – 21:4). Women had few rights in first-century Palestine. On marriage they passed from being the property of their father to being the property of their husband. Their function was to bear children – preferably sons – and if they didn't they could be discarded through divorce.

The scribes love his answer (verse 39) because Jesus seems to confirm their view of the resurrection. And that provokes Jesus to ask a question of his own (verse 41). He focuses on an apparent contradiction in the Scriptures between 2 Samuel 7:12–14 (which says the Messiah will be the son of David) and Psalm 110:1 (which says that he'll be David's Lord). How will the scribes, who applauded Jesus' handling of Scripture a moment ago, deal with this one?

There is no answer, either from the scribes or from Jesus. Clearly, his intention here is to show that the scribes have an inadequate grasp of what the Scriptures reveal about the purposes of God. Luke answers Jesus' question in his second volume, where Jesus, the son of David (1:27, 32–35; 2:4; 18:38–39), is acknowledged as Lord and Messiah through the resurrection and ascension (Acts 2:34–36).

Here the question serves to show that the scribes really can't be relied on any more than the Sadducees as interpreters of Scripture; an opinion driven home by the last part of this section, where Jesus asserts that interpreting

Scripture is only part of the issue anyway. The key thing is to respond to and obey the message of Scripture, something all the leaders of Israel had signally failed to do. (That is the message of the whole of 20:1 – 21:4.)

Jesus turns to his disciples with a warning in a scene reminiscent of 12:1: everyone is listening but his words are specifically for his followers (verse 45). Jesus tells them not to be like the scribes. He condemns them in terms he's used before of his opponents (11:43; 14:7–11). These are people who use religion to feather their own nests and achieve social status. Indeed, they do this at the expense of the poorest of the poor (the 'widow', verse 47). They think their long prayers will get them a blessing. In fact their behaviour will earn them only condemnation.

Then, as if to illustrate his very point, a poor widow comes by and drops a couple of pence into the temple offering box (verses 1–4). This story is often taken as a tale of exemplary, sacrificial giving. And that it is. But it seems, in context, that Jesus' point is the exact opposite. He has come to proclaim a kingdom where widows are supported and helped, not impoverished by a religious exploitation that lines the pockets of the already rich by fleecing the poor, demanding everything they have (12:32–34; 14:12–14; 16:10–13; cf. Acts 6:1–6).

Such a system led by such leaders is ripe for condemnation – something Jesus turns his mind to in the next section. His warning to those of us who follow him is that this is a very real trap that we too could fall into if we lose sight of the values of the kingdom taught by the Scriptures as interpreted by the Son of David, the King of Israel, the Lord of all.

Questions

1. The Bible is the Word of God. Do we need help in interpreting it correctly, or do we believe that any Christian can read it right? What are the right rules of interpretation? (The Crossway Bible Guide series

includes a helpful companion volume on this subject: *The Bible with Pleasure* by Steve Motyer.)

2. Do we ever get sidetracked from the true meaning of the gospel to arguments about points of Scripture or our own opinions and interpretations? How can we live out the heart of our faith and get our doctrine right?

3. How do we read the story of the widow? Should we expect the poor to give sacrificially, or is that just an excuse for the rich to give less?

Luke 21:5–38

Recognizing the times

Christians often get sidetracked into calculating the timetable for Jesus' return. He tells us not to bother. There's a war on; we need to pay attention and stand firm whatever the cost.

The temple in Jerusalem was one of the wonders of the world. Begun by Herod the Great in around 20 BC, it dominated the city, and its golden walls meant that
it was visible for miles. But more than that, the temple was the heart of Jewish national, cultural and religious identity. For them it was the presence of God on earth, the sign of his enduring election of them as his people.

As Jesus teaches, people draw attention to the wonder of the building (verse 5). His response – that its days were numbered (verse 6) – stuns them (verse 7). What follows (verses 8–36) is fraught with difficulty. Is Jesus talking about the fall of Jerusalem, or the end of the world? As ever in Luke, the answer is 'both'. And the key to understanding the section is to remember that Jesus is not giving us a timetable, but alerting his followers to the fact that times ahead will be hard, and telling us how to cope.

Many of his hearers would have assumed that the destruction of the temple would be tantamount to the end of the world, because of the central place the temple had in every Jew's understanding of God and the world. Jesus is at great pains to separate the two events. So he begins with a summary of what's to come (verses 8–11) before fleshing it out in greater detail (verses 12–36).

He warns his hearers to watch out (verses 8, 36), words he's used in relation to the teaching of the Pharisees (12:1, 54–56) and of the disciples' need to look and listen carefully to what is going on around them and to what he's saying (8:16–18; 11:33–36). His words are the ones that matter (verse 33). And he is saying very clearly that the fall of Jerusalem is not the end of the world (verse 9). There will be false prophets saying different things (verse 8) – as indeed happened in AD 66 when the Zealots provoked a revolt that led to Jerusalem's destruction.

In the run-up to the fall of the city, the disciples will face persecution (verses 12–19). There are three things they should know about this in advance. First, it will be an opportunity for witness (verses 13–15; verses 14–15 recall 12:11–12, cf. Acts 6:10). Nevertheless, heartbreaking opposition will come from their own families (verse 16) – hence Jesus' clear teaching about making the kingdom one's prime loyalty (8:19–21; 9:57–62; 12:51–53; 14:26–27). Secondly, it's part of God's plan. Verse 18 recalls 12:7 and gives a picture of being held in the hands of God. Persecution and death are not the end: vindication awaits the faithful – as happened to Jesus himself. And thirdly, because of this, the disciples need to stand firm (verse 19, cf. 9:62; 14:27–35; 18:8).

In verse 20 Jesus answers the disciples' question about the time and the place: 'When you see the soldiers coming, the city will be destroyed,' he says in effect. But this isn't just the result of human action, the Zealot uprising and Rome's response. It is the punishment of God, and it is happening in fulfilment of the Scriptures which have been partially fulfilled once (verse 22, cf. 19:43–44; Jeremiah 5:29; Hosea 9:7; Ezekiel 9:1; 39:33; Daniel 2:44; 8:13–14). The 'times of the Gentiles' (verse 24) refer both to the victory of the Romans in AD 70 and to the proclamation of the gospel to the nations of the world.

Now Jesus' focus shifts to the end of the world (verses 25–28). Introduced with Old Testament pictures of calamity and destruction, Jesus describes his own triumphant and glorious coming in the language of Daniel (verse 27; Daniel 7:13; cf. Acts 1:9–11. See 'The Son of Man', p. 191). But whereas the people of the world will find these days terrifying, the disciples are not to be afraid, because the day when Jesus returns will be the day when they are rescued from the suffering and persecution of this life (verse 28).

He goes on to encourage them to pay attention to what's happening (verses 29–31, cf. 8, 36) and not to get embroiled in the 'business as usual' attitude that has resulted in the current Jewish leadership being caught off guard (verse 34, cf. 12:35–46; 17:24; 19:41–44; 20:9–19). There is an unpredictability about the end of the world that means we always need to be ready (verse 34b) and praying (verse 35, cf. 18:8) that we'll be spared unbearable testing (cf. 22:40, 46).

But what are we to make of verse 32? Did Jesus get the timing wrong, throwing in doubt his assurance of verse 33? No. In Luke, 'this generation' has always meant stubborn, unbelieving people who turn their backs on God's purposes (7:31; 9:41; 11:29–32, 50–51; 16:8; 17:25). There is a 'this generation' in every generation, in all times and in all places. They are the people who resist the good news and oppose God's people.

Jesus' public teaching ministry is now over. Luke concludes this section by recalling his words of 20:1 (verse 37) and telling us the people still find him intriguing (verse 38). The scene is set for the final confrontation between Jesus and the leaders of Jerusalem. The people hope it could still go Jesus' way. We know, from what Jesus has already said, not least in the parable of the tenants, that it cannot.

Questions

1. What lies at the centre of our moral and social universe? How much of a look-in does God get into it?
2. Gather some information and devote some special prayer to situations where verses 12–19 are being acted out today.
3. What does it mean to live now in the light of the fact that Jesus is coming to reign? With what attitudes and actions does he encourage us to face the future?

Luke 22:1–38

A final meal

Throughout his ministry Jesus has done a lot of teaching over the meal table. Now he explains the meaning of his death to his disciples over one last supper.

 The mood significantly darkens with this section. The opposition of the nation's leaders becomes betrayal by friend (verses 1–6) and Jesus' last meal with his disciples is held in an atmosphere brooding with his impending death (verses 7–38). More than that, Satan re-emerges as a key player. Since 4:13 he has been lurking in the shadows; the opposition to Jesus has been human. Now Luke reminds us that behind the animosity of people lies the prince of darkness (verses 3, 31). The conflict Jesus is engaging in is a cosmic one.

For the first time Luke tells us these events are happening at the time of the Jewish festival of Unleavened Bread and Passover (verses 1, 7, 15). Originally two feasts, they had been celebrated together for many years. They both recalled the release of Israel from slavery in Egypt (Exodus 12 – 13). The combined feast was one of three pilgrim festivals in the Jewish calendar (the other two being Pentecost and Tabernacles) that swelled the population of Jerusalem to many times its usual size.

Having warned his disciples that close friends will betray them (21:16), Jesus is now betrayed by Judas, one of the twelve (verse 4). The chief priests and their allies rejoice (verse 5) because they've found a way to get Jesus when the crowds aren't protecting him (verse 6, cf. 19:47–48, 20:19; 21:37–38).

Meanwhile Jesus is making preparations. Note the contrast between James and John, who are doing what Jesus wants them to do (verses 8–13), and Judas, who is planning to betray his master. Note too that Jesus has carefully planned this meal, arranging the use of a room in the city (verses 10–12).

Luke's account of the last supper simultaneously looks back to the exodus and forward to the great banquet (see on 13:22–30; 14:1–24). Aware of the importance of what he's doing, Jesus talks of eagerly wanting to share this last meal with his friends (verse 15), knowing that the events about to unfold will lead to the coming of the rule of God in the lives of all who respond to his apostles' message (verse 13). This is why he speaks of the kingdom (verses 16, 18).

Then he reinterprets key elements of the Passover meal in the light of the exodus he's about to lead through his death (cf. 9:30–31). So the unleavened bread, reminder of the hurry with which the people prepared to leave Egypt, becomes symbolic of his body, broken in martyrdom and sacrifice (verse 19). The wine becomes a picture of his blood poured out in a new covenant (verse 20). The language picks up themes from Jeremiah 31:31–34 and recalls the forgiveness that he offered to those who came to him (e.g. 5:20–26; 7:41–50). Though his death is to the fore, Jesus believes that beyond lies vindication by God because he'll eat and drink with his friends again (verses 16, 18).

This is the destiny that Jesus knows has awaited him

since he set out from Galilee (9:22, 40; 13:33; 17:25; 18:31–33). Yet it has taken people (namely the nation's leaders and Judas) to bring it about, and they must take responsibility for what they do (verse 22). Jesus will not allow anyone to blame God or the devil for what happens in his or her life.

The twelve, however, are more bothered with the seating plan: who's nearest the head of the table (verse 24, cf. 14:7–11). Jesus reminds them of the lessons in leadership he's already given them (e.g. 9:46–48). Then, using language from 17:7–10 and the picture of a child (cf. 9:46–48; 18:16–17), he shows that he has led as a servant and so should the twelve. It is this that will make them able to receive the kingdom and take a lead in it, as the judges did in ancient Israel (verses 29–30).

Mention of trials (verse 28b) leads him to warn the disciples in highly emotional tones about what lies ahead. Satan, having gained the allegiance of Judas already, is trying for the others. Jesus speaks to Peter about all of them (the 'you' in verse 31 is plural), and says that Peter will have a key role in holding the group together and leading it on in the days to come (verse 32). Peter, of course, is having none of it. In a highly ironic show of bravado – ironic because he will indeed be imprisoned and even die for his Lord, but not just yet – he pledges loyalty (verse 33). Jesus predicts disaster (verse 34, cf. 12:8–10), but has already spoken of the possibility of restoration (verse 32b).

As if to bring home the changed circumstances the disciples will find themselves in, Jesus asks them to recall their two missions (verse 35, cf. 9:1ff.; 10:1ff.). They were well received then. They won't be any more. As Jesus is struck down as a lawbreaker by the keepers of the temple, so his followers will be hounded as transgressors. He was known as a friend of sinners (7:34; 15:1–2). Now his friends will be treated as sinners.

They need to be on their guard. But as ever, they are too eagerly literalistic in their response. 'Sword' has been a metaphor for hostility through the gospel (12:51–53; cf. 2:24–25). It is here too. Jesus is not counselling armed resistance; that is ruled out in 6:20–38 and 22:49–51. You can taste the exasperation in his 'That is enough' (38b), with which he brings the conversation and the meal to a close.

Questions

1. In the light of this passage, think about the communion services in your fellowship. What would make them more helpful as a 'remembrance' of Jesus, bringing him close to us now?
2. Is Jesus a pacifist (verse 38, cf. verse 51)? Should we be?
3. The church has divided over the communion or Eucharist more than over anything else. Why is this? Is it right? What can be done?

Table fellowship

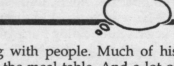

Jesus spent lots of time eating with people. Much of his teaching was delivered around the meal table. And a lot of it concerned who we eat with as well as who'll be eating with him at the great banquet scheduled for the end of history. Dinner parties in Jesus' day were about more than good food and conversation. They were also a sign of who you treated as a friend, 'one of us'. This is an important topic in Luke. Let's take a closer look.

5:27–32	Like a good doctor, Jesus paid house calls.
7:31–35	Jesus has a reputation for eating with the 'wrong' people.
7:36–50	A meal offers the opportunity to contrast polite indifference and true faith.
9:10–17	Jesus hosts a banquet in the desert (with miracles on the menu).
11:37–54	Jesus condemns the Pharisees' table manners.
13:22–30	Jesus spells out who is (and isn't) coming to dinner at the restaurant at the end of the age.

14:1–23	Who should you be inviting for dinner?
15:1–2	The Pharisees condemn Jesus' table manners.
19:1–10	Salvation at the meal table.
22:7–23	A meal to remember the friend of sinners by.

It's not who you meet with but who you eat with that shows who you really accept. How do you put this into practice in your life? And in your church?

Luke 22:39–65

The darkness closes in

Jesus strides out into the darkness to face his severest test. Only prayer will see him and his disciples through what they each have to face. Will we stand in the time of trial?

 Leaving the security and intimacy of the upper room, Jesus and his disciples come out into the open and headlong into the time of trial. Jesus prepares himself through prayer, and urges his friends to do the same (verses 39–46). But when the mob arrives, though Jesus is composed and in control, the disciples are in disarray (verses 47–53) – so much so that while his master is being mocked, Peter is denying all knowledge of him (verses 54–65). This is holy ground we walk on.

Jesus goes to the Mount of Olives (verse 36, cf. 21:37). He has prayed on mountains before (6:12; 9:28), but this place is particularly associated with the coming of the Messiah (Zechariah 14:4). Prayer is the key here (verses 40, 41, 42, 44, 45, 46), not just for Jesus but for the disciples. The time of trial ('temptation', verses 40b, 46b) is upon them, and only prayer will give them the strength to withstand it.

The section recalls the testing in the desert (4:1–13) – the isolation of Jesus, the intense prayer, the ministry of angels. So we can be sure that the devil is active in the testing. The focus here is not on Jesus' identity but on his mission, his taking the 'cup' (verse 42). He has already spelled out what the cup means (19–20), here he reaches the watershed of embracing the will of God which is his destiny, something he can do only because God strengthens him in response to his agonized prayer (verse 43). The intensity of Jesus' praying is seen in his kneeling, which was most unusual (verse 41b), his anguish (verse 44a) and his profuse sweating (verse 44b). In this struggle God provides the resources to go on, not the removal of the trial.

The will of God and what Satan wants coalesce at this moment when Jesus takes the cup of suffering. Satan wants it because he believes it will destroy Jesus. God wants it because he knows that through it Jesus will destroy Satan (cf. 10:18; 11:20–22).

The disciples, overwhelmed by a sense of foreboding and sorrow (verse 45), are asleep. Jesus urges them to wake up and pray (verse 46, cf. 18:11; 21:36). But even as he is doing so, lights appear on the path up from the valley below. A crowd is coming (verse 47a), led by Judas (47b), a friend, who would greet Jesus as a friend (47c).

Others would be thrown by this show of false affection. Not Jesus (verse 48). His time in prayer has left him focused, composed and in control. Note how he takes charge of the encounter so that the mob can't actually arrest him until verse 54. The twelve, of course, are completely thrown by events. The trial has burst upon them and they are anything but composed and focused. They lash out (verses 49–50). Jesus stops them (verse 51a). His ministry is to bring wholeness and healing, even to an enemy (verse 51b).

Now the crowd is identified (verse 52b), and Jesus contrasts himself and his conduct with them and their ways, a contrast thrown into starker relief by the inept action of the disciples (verses 52b–53). Jesus is not a terrorist leading an armed gang; he is a messenger of peace, come to reclaim the allegiance of his people for their God; that's what he was talking about in the temple. The chief priests and their cronies, of course, *are* an armed gang, a bunch of brigands (19:46; 20:47).

Mention of the darkness (verse 53c) carries the suggestion that the leaders were confident to act only after nightfall and in secret. But much more than that, it confirms that this is Satan's moment and that these people are Satan's servants – as we know Judas is (22:3).

Jesus is led away (verse 53a), and the focus shifts to Peter and to his time of trial. He follows, but at a distance (verse 54b). This is half-hearted bravado (verse 33) that results in him sitting around the fire with the enemy. Notice how the time passes (verses 58a, 59a). His denial is no spur-of-the-moment thing. He could have got his courage up, but because of his prayerlessness, it ebbs away as dawn nears. He denies knowing Jesus (verses 56–57); he denies knowing his friends and comrades (verse 58); he even denies his roots in Galilee. Truly he is all at sea and floundering when the cock crows (verse 60).

But even now Jesus, from the midst of his own time of trial, has time for his friend. He looks at him (verse 61a) to remind him of what he had said around the meal table (verses 34, 61b). He demonstrates clearly and very personally to Peter that he is indeed a prophet. Perhaps, in the hours that follow, Peter will recall Jesus' other prophecies concerning his death, and things will begin to fall into place.

Luke reinforces the lesson by immediately telling us that the guards mocked Jesus' prophetic credentials (verse 63), just as Jesus himself said they would (18:31–33). Having called him 'Lord' (verse 61) in the context of remembering a prophetic word, the insults of the guards take on the connotation of blasphemy: this is no mere man they are abusing. But this is only the beginning of Jesus' time of trial. There is more darkness to come.

Questions

---

1. When we pray against temptation, are we asking God to remove the trial or to strengthen us to face it with faith? How can we help our brothers and sisters to do this?
2. When is it right to resist and when to submit to the authorities?
3. How does Peter feel as he denies his Lord? Recall situations when you have reacted as Peter did. How did your faith grow as a result? What would have helped Peter to prepare for his trial?

Luke 22:66 – 23:25

Trial and error

Alone now, Jesus is decisively rejected by his people and condemned by the world; but by embracing his destiny he is about to bring release to all of us.

The trial of Jesus unfolds in four crisp scenes. Jesus himself plays a diminishing role as each scene comes and goes. Before the Sanhedrin he answers  two questions (verses 66–71). Before Pilate he answers one (verses 1–5). Before Herod he is asked a question but remains silent (verses 6–12). On being returned to Pilate, he isn't even addressed (verses 13–25). This hour belongs to the powers of darkness, and they take centre stage – in the Jewish leaders (verses 66, 1–2, 5, 10, 13, 18, 21, 23), in Pilate and Herod, and now even in the people of Jerusalem who had previously sided with Jesus (19:48; 20:19; 21:38) but who now turn on him (verses 13, 18, 23).

The trial before the Sanhedrin sets the agenda for all the other hearings. The issue is Jesus' claim to authority as an alternative to the existing Jerusalem leadership. His accusers are those Jesus predicted would reject him (66; 9:22). And their opening question (verses 67a) strongly echoes Satan's questions in the wilderness (4:3, 9), reminding us that behind those human rulers lie the powers of darkness.

Jesus replies by pointing out that the elders haven't believed anything he's said up to this point (67b–68, recalling especially 20:1–8), and then asserts that whatever people make of him, God will declare him to be king (verse 69). 'Son of Man' (see p. 191) is a title Jesus has used mainly in the context of his rejection (6:22; 7:34; 9:22, 26, 44, 58; 17:24–25; 18:31–33). He uses it here with an echo of Psalm 110:1, the enthronement of the king greater than David (see on 20:41–44).

The elders hear it with an echo of Psalm 2:6–7: the king as God's son (verse 70), which means Jesus is merely claiming to be king, the rightful ruler of Jerusalem who should supplant them from their position of authority. They don't accept this. They believe him to be a false prophet who has led the people astray. We know that the term 'Son of God' means much more than mere 'human king' (e.g. 1:31; 4:31). But they don't. They believe he has condemned himself (verse 71, cf. 11:53–54), and, in setting himself as an alternative to them, he is also challenging Rome. This gives them enough of a case to argue before Pilate. Of course, their actions merely confirm what Jesus said in verse 67b!

Off to Pilate they go, all of them (verse 1), and they arraign him on the charge of being a political subversive and revolutionary (verse 2) from a part of the country noted for breeding trouble-makers (verse 5, cf. 13:1). Their charges are not entirely false. Jesus has claimed to be the king (verse 2c; 19:37–40), the son of the vineyard owner (20:9–19); he was ambivalent about paying taxes (20:20–26), and he is 'subverting' the nation if by that is meant that he is challenging the Sanhedrin's right to lead it in a godly direction.

Pilate smells a rat. His question and Jesus' very direct answer make it clear to him that here is no warrior raising armed rebellion against Roman rule – unlike Barabbas (verse 3). He wants to dismiss the case (verse 4) but the council won't let him (verse 5). Mention of Galilee might have caused him to pause. After all, he's had trouble with Galileans before (13:1). So why not ask Rome's man on the spot (verses 6–7)?

Herod, no doubt in Jerusalem for the feast, has wanted to meet Jesus (verse 8a). In fact, we know he has wanted to kill Jesus for some time (13:31, cf. 9:7–9). Herod clearly isn't siding with the angels. He wants a sign (verse 8b) and Jesus has already condemned those who hunger after signs (11:29–32). So Jesus remains silent (recalling Isaiah's servant, Isaiah 52:13 – 53:12, especially verse 7). The elders constantly make accusations (verse 10), but Herod finds nothing threatening in Jesus. Instead, he mocks him and sends him back to Pilate ironically arrayed as a king (verse 11). Perhaps it is because they reach the same conclusion about Jesus that the two men become friends that day (verse 12).

Pilate wants to deliver his verdict (verse 13). Now for the first time 'the people' appear (verse 13b) – perhaps because the governor wants to test the popular mood to see if it chimes with the wishes of its leaders. He and Herod find Jesus not guilty of the crimes he's accused of (verses 14–15). He is reluctant to continue the trial because, as we're told for the first time, a guilty verdict means death (verses 15b). This raises the stakes considerably and explains why three times Pilate tries to release Jesus (verses 16, 20, 22b). But the crowd will have none of it.

They want Barabbas (verses 18–19, 25). Twice Luke tells us what Barabbas had done, to emphasize the contrast between him and Jesus. He is *really* trying to subvert the state by violent means. He's no friend of Rome and a dubious ally for the Sanhedrin. Yet they cry for his release and for Jesus' death. Truly this is the hour of darkness.

And how ironic that the word 'release' should be so prominent through this final part of the trial story (verses 16, 18, 20, 22c, 25)! Jesus' whole ministry had been about bringing release (4:18–19) to the sick, the poor, the outcast and the demonized. Pilate wants to release Jesus. But in order for Jesus' ministry of release to reach its fulfilment, Pilate must condemn him and release Barabbas. For on the cross Jesus will complete his work of release – the 'exodus' spoken of on the mount of transfiguration (9:31).

So Jesus is condemned by all the powers in the land to face the destiny that he embraced as God's will for him in the garden (22:41–44). Great indeed is the mystery of the kingdom.

Questions

1. Was Jesus the victim of a miscarriage of justice? What can we hope for from human justice? Where is true justice to be found? Should we strive for justice, and who for?
2. Has Pilate received an unfair press from history?
3. Put yourself in the shoes of Jesus' accusers and judges. What was it about Jesus that you find so offensive and perplexing? How do you arrive at your verdict?

The Son of Man

Whenever Jesus spoke about his mission, he referred to himself as 'the Son of Man'. Some scholars have argued that this is just a way of saying 'me', much as members of the British Royal Family refer to themselves as 'one' rather than 'I'. But most agree that the term is derived from Daniel 7:13–14 .

In Daniel 7 the prophet has a vision of beasts that challenge God's authority on earth. These are clearly pictures of human empires arrogantly usurping God's position as ruler. But at the heart of the vision is the enthronement of a human king – referred to as 'one like a son of man' (verse

13) – to whom God gives all authority over the whole earth for ever (7:13–14).

'Son of Man' appears twenty-five times in Luke, always on the lips of Jesus (except 24:7, which is the angels' report of what he said earlier) and always referring to his mission. Jesus seems to have chosen this title as his favoured way of referring to himself precisely because it was not greatly used in discussions about the Messiah in the first century. This meant that Jesus could mould the term exactly to fit his mission. He did this by merging the notions of authority and exaltation contained in Daniel's vision with the humble service and suffering of Isaiah's servant (Isaiah 42:1–9; 49:1–13; 50:4–11; 52:13 – 53:12; cf. 61:1–4).

Jesus uses the term throughout the Gospel, with subtly shifting shades of meaning. Early in his ministry the focus is on authority, particularly for his mission to the poor (see 'Who are the poor?', p. 66). Around the beginning of the travel narrative, the theme of suffering is included. As he nears Jerusalem, he adds the idea of future exaltation and reign to the mix.

▶ **His mission** (7:34; 19:10). The whole reason Jesus came was to reach the lost and poor in keeping with his manifesto of 4:18–19 (Isaiah 61:1–2a).

▶ **His authority** (5:24; 6:5). His mission aroused the interest of the religious leaders of the day early on. As Son of Man he had authority to forgive and to interpret Scripture. Note that these issues were taken up again in his dialogue with Israel's leaders in the temple (20:1–44), and constituted the reason for his arrest (22:66–71).

▶ **His suffering** (6:22; 9:22, 26, 44, 58; 11:30; 18:51; 22:22, 48; 24:7). The trouble with the more common titles for the Messiah – Son of David, Chosen One, Son of God – was that they had no room in them for notions of suffering. Everyone assumed that the Messiah would come, establish the kingdom (probably by defeating the Romans in battle) and rule for ever from Jerusalem. Jesus knew that his mission involved suffering, and so he combined 'Son of Man' with Isaiah's suffering servant to help his disciples grasp this point.

His exaltation (12:8, 10, 40; 17:22, 24, 26, 30; 18:8; 21:27, 36; 22:69). Daniel's human figure ascended to the throne of God to be given dominion over the whole earth for ever. Jesus knew that beyond his suffering lay vindication and authority. But the latter could not come without the former. It would be through suffering that Jesus would release people from sin and the dominion of the powers of darkness (represented in the beasts of Daniel's vision) and bring them into his universal kingdom.

Luke 23:26–56

Crucified, dead and buried

The verdict of the court is carried out. Jesus the prophet, the king on the way to his throne, fulfils his calling to the end by offering forgiveness and salvation to those who see what's happening.

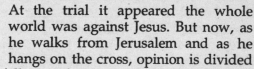

At the trial it appeared the whole world was against Jesus. But now, as he walks from Jerusalem and as he hangs on the cross, opinion is divided again. This section falls into four episodes: the journey to the cross (verses 26–31), the crucifixion (verses 32–43), Jesus' death (verses 44–49) and his burial (verses 50–56). As with the birth of Jesus, so with his death, Luke is less concerned with narrating the details of what happened than with telling us what these events mean.

The condemned man would normally carry the horizontal beam of the cross from the court to the place of execution. For some reason Jesus is unable to carry his; perhaps it is a continuation of the soldiers' mockery that a 'king' should not carry his own burden (cf. verses 36–37). An outsider, Simon from Cyrene (Libya), is pressed into service, and at the outset of the story we have a picture of discipleship: Simon carrying his cross following Jesus (verse 26, cf. 9:23).

Not everyone in Jerusalem approves of the verdict. Women mourn the coming execution (verse 27). But Jesus, who remains composed, focused and firmly believing in God, turns to them with a final prophetic word. Mourn for yourselves and your city, he says; judgment is coming (verses 28–31, cf. 19:41–44). Notice how the Gospel opens with the joy of a barren woman late in life conceiving a messenger of hope (1:5–25), but closes with a word commending barrenness in the light of the coming judgment (verse 29).

Jesus is crucified with others (verses 32–33). These criminals must in some way have been a threat to the state because Rome used crucifixion only as a punishment for rebellion, not for petty theft. Even as the nails are being driven through his wrists, Jesus asks God to forgive his executioners. His ministry is marked to the end by the offer of forgiveness and inclusion to outsiders (verse 34; cf. 1:77; 6:27–36; 7:47–50).

As he hangs on the cross in the morning (possibly around 11am), three groups mock him in highly ironic language. First the rulers – though notice that the people now stand aloof (verse 35), then the soldiers (verses 36–37), then one of the criminals (verse 39). Each of them uses the word 'save' – the very thing Jesus came to do for others (2:11, cf. 9:24). The rulers even call him mockingly the Chosen One (verse 35b, quoting Isaiah 42:1, which God has used of Jesus; 3:22; 9:35). We, the readers, know that Jesus is the Saviour, able to save others; we've read stories of how he's done that right the way through the Gospel. But how does that fit with what we're witnessing now?

Luke answers that question for us in Jesus' encounter with the second criminal and what happens immediately afterwards. The second criminal is the first to see that Jesus won't be saved from suffering but will be vindicated as a result of it. He sees Jesus as innocent (verse 41b), unlike them (verses 40–41a). And he sees that beyond the cross lies the kingdom (verse 42b). It is possible that the word translated 'kingdom' ought to be rendered 'kingly power', for the sense of the criminal's words is that Jesus is heading for his enthronement, his exaltation by God, as Jesus himself confidently predicted at his first trial (22:69).

In repentance, the second criminal asks Jesus to remember him (verse 42a). Even in the midst of his agony, Jesus speaks a word of salvation to the contrite sinner (verse 43). 'Today' speaks of the immediacy of salvation. The paradise that Jesus speaks of lies in the future after his second coming. But the criminal is saved 'now' with a view to being in the kingdom 'then'.

At noon, when the sun should be brightest, the world goes dark. And in that terrifying darkness Jesus engages with the powers that oppose God in such a way that the temple is affected (verse 45b) and a Roman soldier is awestruck (verse 47).

The curtain in the temple hid the Most Holy Place, where the blood of the sacrifice was poured on the altar once a year on the day of atonement. Only the high priest could go in there. So the curtain was the symbol of his power as well as of the gulf that separates God and people. As Jesus hangs on the cross, God rips the curtain open, thus breaking the power of the priests (cf. 20:9–19) and suggesting that the sacrifice being offered on another altar (the cross) is dealing with the sins of all for all time. The Holy Place is now redundant.

At three in the afternoon, Jesus cries in a loud voice and gives his life to God (verse 46). The centurion, who'd been among the mockers (verses 36–37), had received a revelation, for now he sees that Jesus was righteous, and he praises God – a sure sign that he believes God to be at work in what he's just witnessed. Even the people are moved, possibly to second thoughts about Jesus, by what they've seen (verse 48).

The disciples are at a discreet distance. They've been absent from the story until now (verse 49). But Luke tells us they witness what happens. We have to wait for the next chapter to know what they make of it all. Luke particularly draws attention to the women, because they will be centre stage in the opening episode of the next section (verses 49, 55–56; 24:1–12).

Luke ends his account of the crucifixion with a scene of tender kindness that reminds us that not all Jews wanted Jesus killed. The people are as divided over his death as they were over his ministry (cf. 12:51–53). Luke tells us that Joseph was a good man (verses 50–51; only Barnabas gets as good a press; see Acts 11:24). The tomb that Joseph had was probably in preparation for his own burial. The practice was to lay the body there wrapped in linen, covered in spices, for about a year while it rotted. The bones were then gathered into an ossuary and placed in the wall of the tomb.

It is too late in the day to do all the work necessary on the body, so the women go home to prepare the spices they'll need. Everyone rests on the Sabbath (verse 56). The scene is set for what will happen on the first day of the new week. Luke has increased the tension by mentioning the Sabbath twice and forcing us to pause and take stock. How do we respond to the events that have just unfolded before our eyes?

Questions

1. What does Luke's account of the crucifixion tell us about Jesus? (Pay careful attention to what Luke actually says and don't import ideas from other parts of the New Testament.)
2. Do you believe that the rebel on the cross was a genuine convert?

3. What's the significance of the temple curtain being torn and the centurion's confession? What do they tell us about Jesus?

Luke 24:1–35

Unexpected meetings

Nothing could lift the gloom of grief and disappointment from the small band of disciples – except meeting Jesus.

With the crucifixion of Jesus, the adventure is over. The only thing left to do is to complete the burial formalities that were interrupted by the Sabbath (verse 1). Then Jesus' band of followers must rebuild their lives. Indeed, that's possibly beginning, with some already leaving to go home (verse 13). What a shock is in store for them all!

The women, unidentified until verse 10, arrive at the tomb to find it open and empty (verses 2–3). Angels appear, gently rebuking them for looking for the living among the dead (verses 5–6a) and reminding them of what Jesus had told them (verses 6b–7). 'Then they remembered' (verse 8) carries the connotation of revelation: now they see what's happened and understand it. The question is, will any of the others? Needless to say, the eleven disciples dismiss the women's report (verse 11). But something about the way they speak persuades Peter to check it out for himself (verse 12a). His response, however, is not faith but bewilderment (verse 12b).

While this is going on, two disciples are off to Emmaus (verse 13), possibly going home to rebuild their shattered lives. Luke sets this episode up very carefully. It is still the same day, the 'third day' – a fact that assumes greater importance as the story unfolds. The two are on a journey which Jesus will join. Given the importance of journeys already in Luke, we are being prepared for something special to happen. When Jesus joins them (verse 15), they don't see who he is (verse 16) – recalling the lack of insight of the disciples on the road to Jerusalem (see 9:43–45; 18:31–34). The episode ends round the meal table – a place of revelation all through his ministry.

They are surprised by Jesus' lack of knowledge about what has happened (verse 18) – some irony, given their inability to see who he is! Jesus asks them to explain what's happened (verse 19). They talk about Jesus being a prophet (verse 19), even the Messiah (verse 21). But they cannot reconcile their perception of who he was with the fate that has befallen him (verse 20). And they are bewildered by what has happened on this, 'the third day' (verse 21c) – reports of an empty tomb and visions of angels, but no-one seeing Jesus. How ironic again (verses 22–24)!

Jesus chides their lack of faith (verse 25). 'Slow of heart' suggests more than just intellectual failure. These disciples haven't grasped what God is about at all. So he treats them to a Bible study, showing them that suffering was part of the Messiah's calling (verses 26–27). Luke doesn't tell us which scriptures Jesus used. This doesn't matter, because the point being made here is that just as all prophets have suffered (a point Jesus has already made, cf. 11:47–51), so must the Messiah. It is likely, however, that Jesus would have made reference to Isaiah 52:13 – 53:12 and Daniel 7:13–14 because of the importance those texts had for his self-understanding (see 'The Son of Man', p. 191). And it's likely that Psalm 22 (alluded to all through the crucifixion story), Psalm 2:1; 16; 110:1; 118 and Deuteronomy 18:15 would have been included.

This dialogue filled the rest of the journey. They reached their destination and the two urged Jesus to stay with them. Perhaps his words had brought them some comfort; they could continue the conversation over the meal table (verses 28–29). At the meal table, Jesus, the guest, plays the host in a scene reminiscent not so much of the last supper as of the feeding of the five thousand, a scene of revelation for the disciples (verse 30, cf. 9:16–17, 20).

Suddenly the eyes of the two disciples are opened. They recognize him and he vanishes (verse 31), and there's an eruption of joy (verse 32). Everything he's said to them on the road now makes sense not just in their heads but in their hearts (verse 32a). At last they can see who Jesus really was and is. And so they've got to get back to Jerusalem immediately to tell the others. The crucifixion scattered the disciples and threatened to break up the group permanently; the resurrection brings them together as a community of witnesses.

They hurry back (verse 33a) and burst in upon a scene of ecstatic joy. The eleven and the women and others (verse 33b) are excitedly discussing the fact that Jesus has appeared to Simon (verse 34). The two tell the wide-eyed group what happened to them on the road and round the meal table (verse 35). Bewilderment and disbelief – and grief over the tragic and brutal death of their friend and master – have given way to a wondrous joy at all the Lord has done. Truly now they know that Jesus is the Messiah – but what next?

Luke has framed this section quite brilliantly, moving from doubt to faith, from heavy grief to light-headed joy because that is what meeting the risen Jesus does for people. Before we move on to examine the task Jesus gives to his witnesses, we need to ask ourselves whether we have met this risen Messiah.

Questions

1. How do we know that Jesus rose from the dead? What's the basis of our conviction today?
2. Why do you think Jesus stopped the two disciples from recognizing him until the end of the journey? What point does Luke draw out of this (verses 7, 25–27, 32)?
3. Reconstruct the conversation between Simon Peter and

the risen Jesus (verse 34). What did they say to each other?

The kingdom community

Luke stresses that God sent Jesus to fulfil his promise to Abraham that through his family all the families of the earth would be blessed (Genesis 12:1–3; Luke 1:54–55). So it's not surprising that discipleship and mission in Luke are never solo activities. Jesus came to found a new community (6:12–16). What does it look like?

Read the following passages and construct a picture of the new community gathered by Jesus, noting the following (each passage will have information relating to more than one question, so do make some notes):

▶ Who's in it?

▶ How did they get there?

▶ How do they behave towards one another?

▶ How do they treat outsiders?

▶ What are the characteristics of community life?

5:8–11; 27–32; 9:57–62; 18:18–30	Calling disciples, with mixed response.
8:9–10, 16–18; 11:27–28, 33–36; 13:22–30	Listening carefully.
9:1–6; 10:1–24; 24:45–49	Sharing the good news.
6:17–49; 12:22–48; 16:1–31	Hearing the values of the kingdom.
5:29–39; 7:33–36; 14:1; 15:1–2; 22:7–22	Party time in the kingdom.
11:1–13; 22:39–46; 24:25–30, 44–49	The spirituality of the kingdom community.

How does your church measure up against this picture? What are you doing to build a kingdom community where you are?

Luke 24:36–53

Seeing clearly what God has done

Seeing the risen Jesus is only the start. Now the disciples – and we – need to understand what the resurrection means and then go and tell the world.

Luke ends his account with a section that establishes that Jesus has been raised and isn't a ghost (verses 36–43), seals the disciples' understanding of what has happened so they can tell others (verses 43–49) and briefly narrates the ascension (verses 50–53). But many narrative threads are left dangling because Luke wants his readers to go on to volume two, Acts (see Postscript, p. 205).

A hush descends with Jesus' arrival and greeting (verse 36). The disciples are startled, frightened (verse 37), troubled and doubtful (verse 38). It's partly because of joy (verse 41) – it seems too good to be true after what they've been through – and partly because they still don't 'see' the meaning of what's happened.

Jesus' first aim is to assure them that he is no ghost and no mortally wounded but hideously revived cadaver. He is living flesh and blood, raised from death to a new form of bodily existence that enables him to appear and disappear. So he invites them to examine his body with their eyes and hands (verse 39). Then he asks for something to eat because they still can't take it in (verse 41). This he consumes in their presence (verses 42–43).

But the bare fact of his resurrection still isn't enough. The disciples need to be told what it means (verse 44). He repeats what the angel said (verses 6–7) and what he himself said on the road (verses 25–27), demonstrating that Luke thinks this is pretty crucial for us to grasp as well as for the disciples. He reiterates that it is what he said would happen to him (e.g. 9:23; 18:31–33) and that it has all happened because it was written of him in the Scriptures (cf. 22:37).

As he did with the two on the road, so now for the whole group of disciples, he opens their minds to understand the Scriptures (verse 45). He delivers a three-point sermon – the Messiah will suffer, he will rise and repentance and forgiveness will be preached in his name (verses 46–47). Again Luke is not specific about which scriptures Jesus uses. In one sense the whole story of how God will redeem the world from Abraham onwards is in view (Genesis 12:1–3; cf. Luke 1:54–55).

And the climax of this is that repentance and forgiveness will be preached to the ends of the earth (Isaiah 49:6; cf. Luke 2:32; Acts 1:8). Forgiveness has been the crucial content and experience of the salvation Jesus has offered through his ministry (4:18–19; 5:20–21, 23–24; 7:47–49; 11:4; 12:10; 17:3–4; 23:34; cf. Acts 2:38; 5:31; 8:22; 10:43; 13:38; 26:18). And now the disciples will take that message to the world.

They will be witnesses (verse 48). They have seen in two ways and so are able to tell others. First, they've been present at all the key events and can report what they've seen. But secondly, and more importantly, they've 'seen' in the sense of having their minds opened to understand what these events (especially the cross and resurrection) mean. The bare facts are not enough. They need to be interpreted correctly and scripturally.

And just as Jesus was anointed for his ministry (3:22; 4:18–19), so the disciples will be. They will receive power. It is the Father's gift (verse 49b, cf. 11:13; 12:32), but Jesus gives it (verse 49a), and the disciples should wait in the city until the Spirit has come.

So far, everything Luke has told us in this chapter seems to have happened on the same day. Now the timing gets vaguer. Some time later Jesus took his disciples out of the city (verse 50a) and left them for the final time. The ascension story recalls the departures of the great saints of the Old Testament, such as Abraham (Genesis 49) and Moses (Deuteronomy 33).

Like those patriarchs, Jesus imparts a blessing (verses 50–51). This gives his words in verses 44–49 the force of being his last words on earth. That adds a solemnity to the commission he has given his disciples. Then he is taken into heaven to be given the regal power and glory anticipated at his trial and earlier (22:69; 9:26, 32, 51; 19:12). In his departure his disciples see for themselves that God embraces his suffering and reverses the verdict of the human court: truly Jesus is God's Messiah.

How do they respond? They praise God for all he's done through Jesus (verse 53b). They stay in the city in obedience to their master's command (53a). They experience great joy because of what God had done in their midst (52b). But most amazingly of all, they worship Jesus (52a). They see in his ascension the truth that we have known since Luke introduced his characters at the start of his tale: Jesus is the holy one of God, more than a mere man, one who truly merits our worship.

And so his tale ends. But there is a very real sense that this is just the beginning.

Questions

1. What evidence would you use to convince someone that Jesus rose from the dead? (Start with Luke 24, but use other parts of the New Testament as well as your imagination as you reconstruct events and draw conclusions.)
2. Luke emphasizes the role of the Scriptures in enabling us to understand what has happened (verse 46) and what must happen next (verse 47). What does it mean for us,

who weren't there, to be witnesses?

3. Imagine that you have the opportunity to give an Easter address to the General Assembly of the United Nations. What will you say?

Postscript

Beyond Luke's Gospel

Luke has left a number of loose ends. His story is not complete, because his work, uniquely among the Gospel writers, was in two volumes. His Gospel leads us into the Acts of the Apostles in three particularly important ways.

First, the Gospel has said very little about preaching the good news to the Gentiles. That Jesus was born in fulfilment of God's promise to Abraham is clear from the opening episodes (see on 1:5–25, 26–56). This promise was that through Abraham's family all the families on earth would be blessed, and that salvation from sin and its effects would come through his family. This is spelled out by Simeon in the temple when he holds the infant Jesus (2:29–32, quoting Isaiah 49:6).

But Jesus has had very little contact with Gentiles. Aside from the centurion (7:1–10), the demonized man Legion (8:26–39) and the Samaritan leper (17:11–18) no Gentile enjoyed the benefits of his ministry. When he sent his disciples out on mission, it was to Jews only (9:1ff.; 10:1ff.). But his parting words to his followers culminated in the command to be his witnesses to all nations. Acts tells us that story.

Secondly, the Gospel doesn't tell us how the disciples will be empowered to do this job Jesus has given them. There is the promise of the gift of the Holy Spirit but not the fulfilment of that promise (11:13; 24:49). Acts opens with that fulfilment and its consequences.

And thirdly, the Gospel closes without really clarifying the position of Israel. What place does the Jewish nation now have in the plans of God? Some in Israel believed in Jesus (notably the disciples); many rejected him (notably the Jerusalem leaders). Jesus promised salvation for the repentant but judgment on those who failed to recognize who he was. Acts spells out how God's promise to bless the nations affects Israel. (See Simon Jones, *A Rough Guide to the New Testament*, IVP, 1994, pp. 67–87.)

For further reading

There is a wealth of material on Luke's Gospel and the crucial issues it raises. Here's a selection of the best.

Commentaries

Darrell Bock, *Luke* (IVP New Testament Commentary series, 1994). This is a commentary for preachers but also useful for homegroup leaders.

Joel Green, *The Gospel of Luke* (New International Commentary on the New Testament, 1997). This is the most up-to-date and comprehensive commentary by an evangelical on Luke. It is the one that I have leaned most heavily on. It's really for preachers and those familiar with New Testament studies.

Richard Cassidy, *Jesus, Politics and Society: A Study of Luke's Gospel* (Orbis, 1978). An excellent introduction by a Catholic scholar to the social and political effects of Jesus' ministry.

Background books

Joel Green, *The Theology of the Gospel of Luke* (Cambridge University Press, 1995). A first-rate, clear introduction to what Luke teaches us in his Gospel.

Kenneth Bailey, *Poet & Peasant and Through Peasant Eyes* (Eerdmans, 1983). A wonderful discussion of Luke's parables by a scholar who's lived most of his life in the Middle East.